ALABAMA
LORE

THE
CHOCCOLOCCO
MONSTER
HUGGIN' MOLLY
THE LOST TOWN OF
COTTONPORT

and Other Mysterious Tales

WIL ELRICK

THE
History
PRESS

Published by The History Press
Charleston, SC
www.historypress.com

First published 2018

Manufactured in the United States

ISBN 9781467138017

Library of Congress Control Number: 2018936081

Let's keep this book dedication simple: Believe

CONTENTS

Contents

INTRODUCTION

ALABAMA IS A WEIRD
AND WONDERFUL PLACE

If you are reading this, you obviously have an interest in legends and lore, and why wouldn't you? Thousands of years ago, as our ancestors sat around campfires, they told stories. As civilization advanced, people continued to tell tales, but they could also be printed in books to reach more people. Now, with mobile devices, we can literally hold the stories of the world in the palm of our hands—but nothing is quite as satisfying as sitting around a campfire telling a good ol' story. Tales touch us even more when they feature people we know.

What you hold in your hand right now is a collection of tales and legends from around the great state of Alabama. While some are oft-repeated tales easily found in books or on the internet, others required some digging. Some tales developed in recent years, while some are old enough that their origins date to a time when the only technology humans had was firelight. Who knows? You may have told or heard some of these stories yourself around a campfire, on an adventurous retreat or at a fright-filled sleepover. You may have even tried to find the truth behind the legends on a triple-dog dare.

What follows are tales of buried treasures, monsters that roam our woods, vanished towns, unusual places and, of course, plenty of spirits that remain earthbound. There is the story of a famous haunted playground where spectral children play by the light of the moon. Also included are tales about Alabama's ghostly governor, mythical creatures such as Sasquatch and the Wolf Woman of Mobile, a spirit who rocks into eternity

Historic welcome to Alabama sign. *Author's collection.*

in her favorite chair inside her mausoleum and even a witch who wants to hug you to death.

With nearly two hundred years of history, a population large enough to rank the state twenty-fourth in the nation and famous writers with fertile imaginations, Alabama is rife with tall tales, urban legends and folklore galore. From Native American culture, a brutal civil war and two world wars, Alabama has experienced tragedies and triumphs—and left behind stories to tell about it.

Some of the stories contained herein are cautionary tales meant to protect us, others are based on long-held beliefs and some are indicative of our modern society, but all are fun. So sit back and uncover the histories behind the legends that make Alabama such a unique—and weird—place to live.

1

THE STORY OF THE UNION'S LOST GOLD

THE KEEL MOUNTAIN TREASURE

Keel Mountain, near Gurley, has managed to stave off development and remain nearly untouched. Like so many people before me, I believe that the pristine land on Keel Mountain is hiding a secret, one dating back more than 150 years.

In April 1862, Brigadier General Ormsby Mitchel of the U.S. Army made an unexpected and brash maneuver with his Army of Ohio and marched on the city of Huntsville, Alabama, taking the townspeople by such surprise that no one offered resistance. The capture of Huntsville gave the Union army control of most of the larger cities between Huntsville, Alabama, and Nashville, Tennessee.

From his new headquarters in Huntsville, General Mitchel was able to observe the populace of the growing southern city. The Union troops did not witness open rebellion from the townspeople, but they sensed a feeling of unrest that General Mitchel found disconcerting. But he had a more immediate problem—Huntsville lacked a standardized system of currency.

By this point in the war, the Confederate script was useless to the locals, and in any case, Union soldiers would not accept it as a form of payment. But shopkeepers and citizens in Huntsville would not accept the U.S. currency, fearing they would be branded traitors to the Southern cause. General Mitchel was convinced that finding a standard medium of currency would stabilize the local economy and cool some of the resentment toward occupation. So General Mitchel came up with a bold plan: he asked the War Department for $50,000 in gold coins.

Above: Keel Mountain today. *Author's collection.*

Right: Drawing of First Lieutenant William Urlan, Company B, Camp at Huntsville, 1862. *Library of Congress.*

At any other time, this request would have been absurd, but timing and circumstance happened to fall on the general's side. After seizing Huntsville with relative ease, Mitchel was considered something of a hero, and he was promoted from brigadier general to major general. General Mitchel had gained a reputation for leadership, and the War Department granted his request and sent the gold from Washington to the army headquarters in Nashville.

Once the gold was in Nashville, the problem became how to get the gold to Huntsville. Mitchel assembled a small unit from his Fourth Ohio Cavalry division and devised a plan to sneak through the countryside to Nashville, collect the gold and secret it back to Huntsville. Army leaders thought the smaller unit would stand a better chance of avoiding Confederate cavalry or one of the guerrilla units that roamed the low, rolling hills of northern Alabama and southern Tennessee.

It was mid-September when the detachment of heavily armed cavalry troopers left Huntsville for Nashville. The group was led by a first lieutenant and consisted of a sergeant and nine enlisted cavalry soldiers. This small group was able to navigate its way to military headquarters in Nashville with few problems. Once at the camp, the soldiers rested and agreed to set out for Huntsville with the gold at the next nightfall.

The next night, the soldiers loaded the gold coins into two large leather bags and put them in strongboxes, which they fastened securely to a pack mule. One of the enlisted cavalry troopers would lead the mule behind his horse. The soldiers then set out for the return trip, but this part of the journey would not go as smoothly.

It was near the town of Belleview that the Union soldiers encountered their first problem—one of the group's scouts reported a Confederate cavalry detachment camped west of the town. The lieutenant, attempting to avoid the Confederates, moved his troops east toward Booneville to take a different route. But this course led them into the path of a group of Southern guerrillas hidden in a tree line, and the Rebels opened fire on the Union soldiers.

The Union soldiers fled the firefight as fast as their horses could gallop, stopping a few miles down the road to set up an ambush for the guerrillas following them. Four of the Union troopers took a defensive position while the rest of the detachment continued south, protecting the gold. The Union troopers were able to kill several of the guerrillas but three of the four Union soldiers were killed in the battle. The remaining soldier caught up with his group near Fayetteville, which happened to be where they encountered a much larger group of Confederate marauders.

This time, they avoided being spotted by the new band of guerrillas by riding through woodland trails, but when they got back on the road, they ran directly into the guerrillas' scouting party. The troopers were able to kill one of the guerrillas, but one escaped and warned his band of thirty men. The men chased the small Union detachment, which was riding furiously toward the state line at Old Elora Place.

Crossing into Alabama, the Union soldiers thought they had lost their pursuers and went through New Market, heading for Lewis Mountain and the Flint River. They thought they would be able to follow the river south to the Union outpost at the John Gurley farm, but little did they know, they had been spotted by a third group of Confederate guerrillas who had a hideout in the nearby valley known as Potts Hollow.

The guerrillas from Tennessee were also catching up to the Union troopers, who were now being charged on two sides. This left the lieutenant with only one choice. He ordered his men to ride up the slope of Keel Mountain, which was looming in front of them. He thought that if they could make it to the top and set up a defensive position, Union troops from the other side of the mountain would hear the firefight and come to their rescue.

Union soldiers on Lookout Mountain. *Library of Congress.*

Rendition drawing of the camp of General Alexander McDowell McCook near Stevenson, summer 1862. *Library of Congress.*

As the soldiers were riding up the mountain, the guerrillas began firing on them, killing one trooper and the pack mule carrying the gold coins. The trooper leading the mule jumped off his horse and cut the boxes loose from its back. He took the leather satchels out of each box and began dragging them up the slope of the mountain. A round from the guerrillas struck the trooper in the neck, mortally wounding him and knocking him into a depression—along with the coins. His weight, combined with that of the coins, pushed him to the bottom of the hole; the leaves then covered his body, making him virtually undetectable.

This is where we meet the man at the crux of this story: sixty-year-old Jeremiah McCain. The guerrillas continued to force their way up the mountain after the federal troopers, oblivious to the fallen soldier and the gold—all of the guerrillas, that is, except for Jeremiah McCain. McCain had seen the trooper fall and went into the hole to plunder the body. Imagine McCain's surprise when he opened the bags and discovered the gold coins. Being greedy and having no desire to share his newly discovered treasure, he buried the satchels in a hole near the top of the mountain and covered it with stones and leaves. He then counted off exactly seventy-six paces from a nearby oak tree.

Jeremiah McCain survived the skirmish on Keel Mountain, as did most of the guerrillas. Only two of the Union troopers survived to make it back to Huntsville to report the lost gold. General Mitchel was irate at the loss of so much gold and sent several patrols and search parties to Keel Mountain in search of the treasure, but it was never recovered. The army eventually wrote off the gold as being stolen by the Confederates. Mitchel also sent armed patrols to capture any Confederate marauders in the area, and this is how Jeremiah McCain met his fate. Before he was able to return for his gold, he, along with several other guerrillas, were attacked by Union forces near New Market.

During this skirmish, McCain took a bullet to the stomach, and like so many others who had been gut-shot, caught an infection and died a slow, painful death. On his deathbed, he tried telling one of his comrades of the existence and location of the gold, but in his pained and delirious state, his story was unintelligible. Still, people knew the gold had last been seen on Keel Mountain, and the story was passed from one generation to the next. In the last century and a half, many have searched for the treasure, which is now worth $1.5 million.

How much of this story is true? The occupation of Huntsville by General Mitchel, the need for currency and the presence of numerous bands of guerrillas in rural Alabama and Tennessee were real. And one of the groups did include a man named Jeremiah McCain. But the story of the gold? It is repeated often in the South, listing differing cities where the stash may have been lost. There are also plenty of stories about Southerners who hid their gold from Union troops, and in at least one case, a Civil War treasure was discovered.

It happened near Demopolis, Alabama, in 1926. Newspaper accounts at the time reported that Gayus Whitfield found gold hidden by his grandfather General Nathan Bryan Whitfield, using a map left to Gayus by his father, Boaz Whitfield. The general was "one of the richest of Alabama's pre-war citizens," according to an Associated Press story, and the builder of the Greek Revival mansion called Gaineswood that today is a museum offering tours.

What did the general's grandson discover in 1926? Gold worth $200,000, which would be more than $2.6 million today. It was discovered eighteen miles from Demopolis "in an old powder can which crumbled at touch."

Did You Know

Dan Sachs wrote a song, "Lost Keel Mountain Gold," about the lost treasure.

2

THE LEGEND OF
THE MISER'S GOLD

The legend of a miserly north Alabama man is reminiscent of the Charlie Daniels song "The Legend of Wooley Swamp":

People didn't think too much of him
They all thought he acted funny
The old man didn't care about people anyway
All he cared about was his money.
He'd stuff it all down in Mason jars and bury it all around
But on certain nights if the moon was right
He'd dig it up out of the ground.
He'd pour it all out on the floor of his shack
And run his fingers through it.
Old Lucias Clay was a greedy old man
And that's all there ever was to it.
Copyright © Universal Music Publishing Group

The gentleman in the Alabama story is one C.S. Sharps, who was a businessman in Lauderdale County in the late 1890s. Not only did he mistrust the bank, but he also had a quirk—he would only accept payment in the form of gold coins. Every few weeks, he'd take the accumulated coins and bury them in the woods near his gristmill just outside of Florence.

Sharps was already established as a businessman when he purchased the White Mill in 1897. It was one of the oldest in the area and had been

Above: Northeast view of Florence, June 22, 1862. *Library of Congress.*

Left: Man with shovel. *Library of Congress.*

profitable under the ownership of Sherwood White. Sharps, a consummate businessman, planned to make it even more successful.

Located on Second Creek in the eastern portion of the county, the mill was already being utilized by many area farmers to grind corn for their personal use. Soon, Sharps began buying crops from local farmers and grinding them into flour, which he would then sell back to the people in the area. It was profitable for everyone: the farmers had more opportunity to sell crops, additional local people were put to work in the mill, the residents could purchase cheaper flour and Sharps watched the money roll in. His system was working so well that he purchased one hundred acres of nearby forest to clear and plant new crops.

Now remember, Sharps was eccentric. As he obtained more and more gold coins, Sharps became the subject of rumors, as people made guesses about what he did with his fortune. They could only guess, until one day, when a young man working at the mill came forward with an outrageous story. That man was Sharps's nephew Grady, who was the mill bookkeeper.

Grady told several locals that every week, his uncle would count the gold he had taken in during the week and then put it in old feed sacks. He would then secretly take the bags into the woods when he thought no one was around. On more than one occasion, Grady followed Sharps into the woods, but knowing the old man's temper, he would never follow too closely for fear of discovery. He never got close enough to determine where he was taking the sacks of gold.

After a couple of years, Sharps decided to use some of his profits to make much-needed repairs to the mill and upgrade some equipment. He hired crews of men to do the work while he oversaw the projects.

While supervising a crew on the roof one day, Sharps lost his footing and slid down the sloped roof. Several of the workers tried to grab the old man, but none was successful. He fell into the retention pond below. Sadly, he was unable to swim, and even though some of the workers jumped in after him, C.S. Sharps drowned in the pond beside his mill.

After Sharps's death, Grady made hundreds of trips into the woods surrounding the mill searching for the gold he was sure was buried there. He never found it. Before his death, he passed his story on to local residents, many of whom also spent countless hours in the woods looking for C.S. Sharps's buried gold. To this day, no one has admitted to finding the stash.

The tale of C.S. Sharps is another in a long line of stories I have come across in my quest for tales of buried treasure. After digging into the archives, I can only prove parts of Sharps's story. The old mill does exist, and much of the surrounding area has been undeveloped for the last 115 years. Several locals told me they knew of the legend of the gold and have sometimes gone to look for themselves. If half a lifetime of research has taught me anything, it's that every legend has to start with some grain of truth. Since the old White Mill exists, it seems possible the gold does as well.

MORE TALES OF BURIED TREASURE IN ALABAMA

The lost gold of Keel Mountain, the hidden gold of C.S. Sharps and the fabled Cherokee treasure of the Paint Rock Valley are some of Alabama's most well-known treasure tales. But if legends are to be believed, numerous counties across the state have buried gold. For the adventurous, treasure-hunting spirit in all of us, here is a short list of more places you can search:

HARDY CLEMONS'S GOLD NEAR TUSCALOOSA: Clemons was the wealthy owner of a plantation near Big Sandy Creek. Legend says that when the Civil War reached Alabama, he was concerned Union troops would find his money, so he buried about $100,000 in gold somewhere on his property. Clemons died in 1863 without revealing the location of the gold. Rumors say that it could be buried under his house, around the cotton gin near the spring, near the old hog farm or in the slave cemetery.

JOHN WILLSMITH'S TREASURE IN FORT PAYNE: In the late 1800s, Willsmith owned half of the town of Fort Payne. Rumors circulated that he kept a large cache of gold coins buried on his property because he did not trust the bank. Willsmith died in 1898, and immediately following his death, many searchers looked for the treasure without success.

THE TREASURE OF BUZZARD ROOST IN COLBERT COUNTY: In the early 1800s, a man named Levi Colbert, who operated a ferry on the Tennessee River, is said to have buried large amounts of gold and silver coins east of his house in the area known as Buzzard Roost. It is just off of the Natchez Trace Parkway near the Tennessee River.

HICKSON'S GOLD IN BRIDGEPORT: Little is known of the story behind this legend, but for more than one hundred years, locals have talked about a treasure consisting of more than $30,000 in gold coins buried somewhere in the town.

RAILROAD BILL'S LOOT NEAR ATMORE: Notorious outlaw Morris Slater, better known as Railroad Bill, was a train robber and thief who operated in south Alabama. The man was real, but he grew into a legend—people said he turned into animals such as rabbits or birds to escape capture. Bill was seen as a Robin Hood–style vigilante who stole from the rich and gave to the poor communities in southern Alabama and northern Florida, although his motives proved to be more selfish. He was wanted for more than six years before he was gunned down while exiting a store in Atmore in 1896. None of his loot was ever recovered, and for more than one hundred years, it has been whispered that his treasure was buried in a cave somewhere near Atmore. Railroad Bill left a possible clue to this treasure when he once said he never strayed far from the railroad tracks between Atmore and Bay Minette.

THE CONFEDERATE GOLD OF ATHENS: In 1865, Confederate forces were transporting a large cache of gold coins to Columbia, Tennessee, when the wagon carrying the gold became mired in a bog hole near Athens in Limestone County. As soldiers were trying to free the wagon, they noticed approaching Union forces, so the guards quickly buried the boxes to keep them out of Union hands. The reported $100,000 of coins were being transported in two wooden crates measuring two feet by three feet by four feet. The crates were reportedly buried near a stream about four miles north of Athens and about half a mile west of the crossing. To this date, the treasure has not been recovered.

3

THE MANY LEGENDS SURROUNDING FAMED AUTHORS HARPER LEE AND TRUMAN CAPOTE

For the aspiring writer or the veteran wordsmith, there is no more legendary city in Alabama than Monroeville. In addition to being the childhood home of Truman Capote, the town was also the birthplace of Harper Lee and the inspiration for the setting of her Pulitzer Prize–winning novel, *To Kill a Mockingbird*.

Being home to two of American literature's most prominent writers gives the town iconic status. It has long been legend that visiting the tiny town and drinking the water will do wonders for your writing. Could there be truth to the idea that something in the water or the air spawns great writers?

Historical marker at the boyhood home of Truman Capote in Monroeville. *Author's collection.*

There is still more to give credence to the legend: Monroeville has also been home to contemporary writers, including *Crazy in Alabama* author Mark Childress, syndicated columnist and author Rheta Grimsley Johnson and Pulitzer Prize–winning columnist Cynthia Tucker. In 1997, the Alabama legislature designated Monroeville and Monroe County as the "Literary Capital of Alabama."

While the "there's something in the water" legend clearly stems from wishful thinking, other tales involving the city's famous residents have definitive answers. The legends say:

1. Truman Capote helped Harper Lee write *To Kill a Mockingbird* or wrote it for her.

2. Truman and Nelle Harper Lee, who grew up to write about murders, befriended a future murderer when they were children.

3. After being friends for much of their lives, Truman and Nelle were enemies at the time of his death in 1984.

To tell those stories, I have to set the scene. Visiting the small Black Belt town of Monroeville is like taking a step into the pages of Lee's great American novel. Even today, readers would recognize the town from young Scout's description of her hometown. The old Monroe County courthouse inspired the one in Maycomb where the fictional Atticus Finch practiced law. It is easy to imagine Scout and her friends playing in the quaint neighborhoods.

Monroeville officials and residents actively promote the town's literary ties. A bronze sculpture in front of the historic courthouse shows three children reading a copy of *To Kill a Mockingbird* on a bench, a tribute to Lee, her novel and the joys of reading. The sculpture was created by Birmingham artist Branko Medenica and installed in 2014. Another monument on the courthouse grounds, installed by the Alabama Bar Association, is a tribute to fictional legal hero Atticus Finch.

Businesses also pay homage to *Mockingbird* with murals adorning several downtown buildings. Each year, a local acting troupe known as the Mockingbird Players brings the novel to life at the old courthouse, with the dramatic trial taking place in the historic courtroom where Lee's father, Amasa Coleman Lee, practiced law.

Truman Capote moved to Monroeville from New Orleans when he was five to live with his mother's cousins. He and Lee became fast friends. Lee

The Old Monroe Courthouse was the inspiration for the Maycomb Courthouse in *To Kill a Mockingbird*. *Author's collection*.

A mural depicting a scene from *To Kill a Mockingbird* on the side of a building in downtown Monroeville. *Author's collection*.

said she was a tomboy and often played the role of protector to the differently dressed and out-of-place Capote while growing up. During their childhoods, the friends developed a love of books by reading aloud to each other. Lee's father noticed their mutual love of reading and gave them a typewriter to share. The two spent hours with one dictating stories while the other typed.

As adults, the writers paid tribute to each other in their works. Lee based her character Dill on Capote, while Capote based the *Other Voices, Other Rooms* character Idabel Thompkins on Lee.

Capote died in Los Angeles, California, on August 25, 1984, but the complicated man is still fondly remembered in Monroeville and featured in numerous exhibits in the Monroe County Museum.

After the 1960 publication of *To Kill a Mockingbird*, Lee wrote a handful of essays before retreating from public life. In 2007, Lee was the recipient of the Presidential Medal of Freedom for her contributions to literature. But it wasn't until 2015, when she was eighty-nine years old, that her second book, *Go Set a Watchman*, was released. She died a few months later, on February 19, 2016, in Monroeville.

Now to address the legends mentioned earlier:

1. According to the Monroe County Museum website, a letter in its collection written by Capote proves he didn't help Lee write *Mockingbird*.

The legend arose after Lee's book was met with immediate and wild success. She was quiet and unassuming while Capote was flamboyant and sought the spotlight. He was known as a brilliant writer and controversial figure in American literature, with more than forty works to his credit, including *Breakfast at Tiffany's*, *Other Voices, Other Rooms*, *The Grass Harp*, *A Christmas Memory* and the renowned nonfiction novel *In Cold Blood*. Because Lee seemed to be a "one-hit wonder," some people assumed she didn't have the ability to write another book.

But the letter at the museum, written in July 1959 by Capote to his aunt Mary Ida in Monroeville, shows he had nothing to do with *Mockingbird*, which was published the next year.

It says:

Yes, it is true that Nelle Lee is publishing a book. I did not see Nelle last winter, but the previous year she showed me as much of the book as she'd written, and I liked it very much. She has real talent. Oh, I do wish I could have some butterbeans. Now! This very minute. Love to all, hugs and kisses, T.

In fact, the opposite seems to be the case—Lee helped Capote with his writing several times. She went to Kansas to help him research *In Cold Blood* and spent months with him, interviewing locals and taking copious notes. In addition, Capote was known as such an attention seeker that people doubt he would have let Lee take the credit for the Pulitzer Prize–winning book if he'd helped her or written it on his own.

2. Yes, Lee and Capote befriended a future murderer as children.

According to Marja Mills in *The Mockingbird Next Door: Life with Harper Lee*, the pair met a little girl visiting the town in 1936, when Lee was ten and Capote was twelve. That summer, a young girl named Martha was visiting a family who lived across the street. Young Truman, reportedly infatuated, planned to run away with Martha, and the two actually managed to hitchhike to the town of Evergreen before a hotel clerk became suspicious of children traveling alone and reported them. Years later, Lee and Capote would learn that Martha Beck and her partner, Raymond Fernandez, had been luring young women using personal ads and brutally murdering them. The couple became known as the Lonely Hearts Killers and were executed in 1951.

3. Lee and Capote did become estranged. By the time Capote died, Nelle was no longer speaking to him, in part because he was a selfish and jealous man.

In Wayne Flynt's *Mockingbird Songs*, he shares a letter in which Lee wrote, "I was his oldest friend, and I did something Truman could not forgive: I wrote a novel that sold. He nursed his envy for more than 20 years." But Capote's biggest sin, one the Lee family couldn't forget, was a claim he made about Lee's late mother, Frances Finch Lee. Capote said Frances had twice tried to drown Nelle in the bathtub, an allegation Nelle and her sister Alice vehemently denied, according to *The Mockingbird Next Door*.

To get a feel for how the two future literary stars spent their childhood, visit Monroeville to tour the sites of their former homes and visit the museum. It's easy to picture the innocent days of their youths, before fame took their lives down unexpected paths.

4

THE GHOSTS OF THE MIGHTY
ALABAMA

Viewed from the shores of Mobile Bay, the sleek lines of the USS *Alabama* recall an era when the majestic battleship led a wartime fleet. Some say the ship's activities in World War II left behind a negative energy that haunts the ship today. Visitors report hearing footsteps walking nearby but say when they turn toward the noise, no one is there. Others claim to have seen apparitions in the cooks' galley as well as the officers' quarters. A common report is that the ship's massive steel doors will close on their own. Who, or what, still lurks in the hull and passageways?

Today, the USS *Alabama*, docked in the bay as a floating museum since 1965, is a source of state pride and one of the most visited tourist attractions in the state, with more than fifteen million visitors since opening. Among the guests are those who claim to have seen more than massive guns and military artifacts, leading to legends that the ship is haunted.

The ship, also known by the designation BB-60, is the sixth U.S. Navy vessel to bear the name *Alabama*. The South Dakota–class battleship was commissioned in 1942. At the commissioning ceremony on August 16, 1942, Secretary of the Navy Frank Knox said:

> As *Alabama* *slides down the ways today, she carries with her a great name and a great tradition. We cannot doubt that before many months have passed she will have had her first taste of battle. The Navy welcomes her as a new queen among her peers. In the future, as in the past, may the name* Alabama *ever stand for fighting spirit and devotion to a cause.*

The USS *Alabama* docked in Mobile as a floating museum. *Author's collection.*

The *Alabama*, nicknamed the "Mighty A," served the next three years in the North Atlantic and South Pacific theaters. During this time, as home to more than 2,500 sailors, it ran hundreds of missions, saw heavy combat, fired more than 1,250 16-inch shells on the enemy during supporting bombardments, shot down twenty-two enemy aircraft and earned nine battle stars for Meritorious Service. *Alabama* ended its wartime service after leading the American fleet into Tokyo Bay on September 5, 1945, having never incurred any damage from enemy action. Even more impressive, during the battleship's thirty-seven months of World War II service, no sailors were injured by enemy fire. Because of this feat, the *Alabama* was also called the "Lucky A."

The only wartime casualties to occur on its decks were due to an accidental explosion on February 21, 1944, when one of the gun mounts inadvertently fired into another gun mount. Five men perished, and eleven more were injured. But the sailors weren't the only ones killed aboard the Lucky A—two men were reportedly killed inside the ship while it was being built at the Norfolk Naval Shipyard in Virginia. Some people believe the spirits of these men were so devoted to the ship that they never left, particularly because reports of ghostly footsteps and shadowy figures

The USS *Alabama* at sea. *Wikimedia Commons.*

below decks predate the ship's conversion to a museum. In fact, numerous servicemen filed reports of weird occurrences aboard ship.

During its time as a museum, the USS *Alabama* has been the subject of numerous tales of hauntings. A website dedicated to recording paranormal experiences posted this anonymous report from March 2017:

> *First of all, I've visited this place a million times. One time after I went below deck after just boarding the museum ship, I heard gunshots. And I mean loud, extremely real, like gunshots from outside. I also heard men yelling unrecognizable words, one I could make out was "fire!" I reacted by dropping to the floor and covering my ears. My dad looked at me like I was crazy, and by that time, the noise stopped. I asked if he heard the guns and his eyes widened and he said no. I then ran up the stairs to the outside deck. All I saw was tourists and visitors walking around. I was the only one that heard it. It scared me bad.*

Reports like that one lure paranormal researchers to the USS *Alabama*, but staff members say the ship is not haunted and that no one who has ever stayed the night on the floating museum reported ghostly encounters.

A battleship firing its main guns on an unknown mission during World War II. *Wikimedia Commons.*

Because of this, Battleship Memorial Park administrators do not allow paranormal investigations aboard the ship. Anyone interested in seeing the ship for themselves can do so during the day, with paid admission. Those hoping to spend the night are out of luck—only employees and youth groups with special permission are allowed to visit after regular hours.

If you visit the battleship, be sure to check out the other attractions in Battleship Memorial Park, including the submarine USS *Drum*, aircraft and tanks and a veterans' memorial, all of which combine to make the park a recognizable symbol of the bravery of those who served our country—the living and the dead.

5

WHEN UFOs VISITED THE TINY TOWN OF FYFFE

The Friday before Valentine's Day in 1989 was a routine one for two law officers in the small Alabama town of Fyffe—until a local woman called to report a strange, lighted object she'd seen in the sky. Police Chief Charles Garmany and Assistant Police Chief Fred Works responded to her call, not realizing their names would soon be cemented in Alabama lore.

Fyffe, located along Alabama Highway 75 between Albertville and Rainsville, had a unique history even before the sightings began that February. Formed in the late 1880s, the town of a few hundred residents remained unnamed until the turn of the century. When mail service was needed to the area in the early 1900s, the U.S. Post Office suggested the name Fyffe, which the town fathers adopted. The small community slowly grew atop Sand Mountain until it was finally incorporated in 1956. Despite the glare of the spotlight it would soon experience, Fyffe would remain a close-knit community.

Garmany and Works, determined to check the woman's claim, drove along County Road 43. The pair soon spotted lights in the sky, just as the caller described, and pulled over. Exiting the patrol car, the men saw a triangular metallic object, which they would later describe as "bigger than a jumbo jet" and eerily silent. Over the next forty-eight hours, more than fifty people in Fyffe—or approximately 2.5 percent of the population at that time—reported similar visions of the unknown objects. The object was described as hovering "at an angle from 1 o'clock to 7 o'clock with bright lights at the top and bottom. The curvature was outlined in green with a real

Were alien spacecraft really sighted in the sky above Fyffe? *Author's collection.*

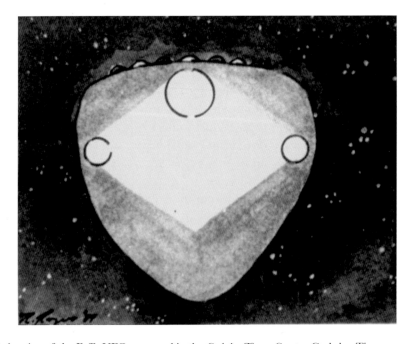

A drawing of the Fyffe UFO appeared in the *Gadsden Times*. *Courtesy* Gadsden Times.

bright light in the center." The reports found legitimacy in the corroboration of more law officers, policemen from Crossville and Geraldine, as well as an Alabama state trooper.

It didn't take long for reports to reach the media. Soon, more than four thousand tourists and representatives from one hundred news agencies poured into the small town. Town businesses and restaurants were booming, and some fast-thinking entrepreneur began selling T-shirts with the slogan "I Survived the Fyffe UFO." Even the *New York Times* covered the story:

> *FYFFE, Alabama—The prospect of seeing a UFO lured more than 4,000 people to this town of 1,300 in northeast Alabama Friday night, but for all the hoopla no unidentified flying objects were sighted. Visibility was difficult because of clouds and light rain. Fyffe got on the UFO circuit Feb. 10, when a woman reported seeing a strange light in the sky and the police later reported seeing a large lighted object passing silently over them. Numerous other sightings have been reported since then.*

Not since the 1947 incident in Roswell, New Mexico, had a UFO sighting in the United States gained so much notoriety. Roswell would later be billed as the site of "the world's most famous, most exhaustively investigated, and most thoroughly debunked UFO claim."

Speculation about the Alabama sightings was wide and varied: Some said the object was an undercover government plane; others thought it could be a heavenly body, a weather balloon (the popular excuse for the Roswell sightings) or even an optical illusion. The source stumped spectators and scientists alike, as the UFO continued to make appearances for more than a month. The weather balloon theory was soon put to rest, as officials with the National Scientific Balloon Facility revealed their project had ended the year before, and they could account for all of their balloons.

For weeks, tourists and reporters continued to come to Fyffe, where the phenomena appeared between 6:00 p.m. and 11:00 p.m. almost nightly. While many of the sightings are still without explanation, some were later explained as aircraft operating in the area. After a couple of months of booming tourism, the interest in the Fyffe UFO began to wane, and residents and local police officers became tired of the ever-growing jokes at the town's expense.

More than a decade after the national limelight shined on this small mountain hamlet, town officials decided to revisit their claim to fame by establishing an event called Fyffe UFO Days, but in this case, UFO stood for "Ultimate Family Outing." Events include arts and crafts vendors, live music, children's activities and a hot air balloon festival. Despite this light-hearted response to its fame, questions surrounding the Fyffe UFO sightings remain, and from time to time, UFO hunters can still be found searching the skies from the top of Sand Mountain.

While Fyffe may have received recognition as Alabama's UFO capital, it is not the only location to report unusual sightings in the skies. Unidentified objects have been reported in the skies over Falkville (1973), Moundville (1976), Hayden Mountain (1977) and Tuscaloosa (1977). The Mutual UFO Network (MUFON) routinely ranks Alabama among the top twenty states with the highest number of annual UFO sightings. Some folks on and around Sand Mountain believe UFOs continue to visit the area, but after all of the scrutiny heaped on Fyffe, residents are less inclined to bring them to the attention of the public.

6

THE GHOSTS OF OAKEY STREAK

In several years of searching out haunted places in Alabama for various writing assignments, I have discovered many little-known haunts and have learned to take the stories of these places and all paranormal places as often exaggerated tales of local lore. This was especially true of what has often been referred to as "the most haunted place in Alabama" or "the most haunted place no one has ever heard of." The name of the haunted location was Oakey Streak Church and Cemetery. It's true, I had never heard of it, and if all of the legends surrounding the place were true, it would be considered the most haunted place in the United States.

Oakey Streak Methodist Episcopal Church is much like any other country church, with a white clapboard exterior, simple steeple and Gothic-style windows. The adjoining cemetery is tidy and filled with simple markers. Nothing about the place indicates how it got its reputation as the most haunted place in Alabama or the most haunted place no one has heard of. After years of visiting reportedly haunted sites in Alabama, I knew to take the legends with a bit of *Scooby-Doo*–style skepticism.

The congregation at Oakey Streak, named for the rows of huge live oaks in the area, was organized in 1831 in a corner of Butler County near Red Level. The land where the current building is set was given to the church in 1851. A log building was initially erected on the land, but it was replaced by the current frame structure around the 1880s. The church was expanded with the addition of a bell tower in 1903. A Masonic lodge was constructed alongside the church, but it was demolished in the

Is the Oakey Streak Methodist Church haunted? *Author's collection.*

1940s, leaving the church as the social center of the area. The church's congregation is still active today.

Oakey Streak Church and its cemetery are unusual because people have reported nearly every element of paranormal activity imaginable, all in one spot.

- ghost children, check
- ghosts of Civil War soldiers, check
- mysterious lights, check
- a mysterious vehicle that follows visitors before disappearing (also known as a ghost rider), check
- mysterious wailing and other noises, check
- Gaelic banshee, check
- grave of someone who died on Friday the 13, check
- graves of unknown dead, check
- ghosts of slaves, check
- hellhounds, check
- the sounds of disembodied footsteps, check
- sudden deaths from hauntings, check
- a haunted outhouse, check

As ridiculous as many of items on the list may seem, reports for all can be found online, albeit with little or no foundation.

After reading all these tales, I decided I needed to see the church and cemetery myself. Finding it proved difficult, because it is described as being in Red Level but it is actually in a rural community. When I did arrive, I was expecting to see a scary-looking rundown shack of a church and a graveyard worthy of a *Scooby-Doo* episode. Instead, I found the quaint and well-kept church surrounded by oaks.

As soon as I began walking around the grounds, my stomach filled with a fluttering throng of butterflies that refused to be calmed. A terrible feeling washed over me like a wave. I have been to hundreds of haunted locations and never had feelings like this. Walking into the cemetery was like walking into the Arctic it felt so cold, still and isolated. In addition, I felt as if I were being followed the entire time I was inside the cemetery fence. My wife, who was along for the ride, was suffering none of these effects and calmly strolled among the graves. At this point, I took a deep breath and steadied myself, thinking perhaps the stories had gotten to me. Suddenly, I heard soldiers marching along the asphalt road. As difficult as it was to appear normal, I managed to take photos of the church, cemetery and individual graves before packing up and getting the heck out of there.

Was my experience unusual? Let's look at the rumored hauntings and see what's been said about the most haunted place in Alabama.

- According to internet reports, two ghostly children make appearances at Oakey Streak. The first is the spirit of a little boy who arrives with a wash of cold air and sometimes rolls a ball toward you as if he wants to play. The second is the figure of a little girl who skips along an access road between the church and cemetery. Legend says vehicles stall when they try to pass the girl's apparition.

- Legend says the ghosts of Civil War soldiers march across these grounds. Although I could have sworn I experienced this phenomenon myself, there is no real evidence. Only a handful of Confederate soldiers are buried in the cemetery, at least in marked graves, and most didn't die during the conflict.

- Witnesses say floating balls of light can be seen around the cemetery and church.

- The oddly specific ghost rider legend says if you park at the cemetery and stay in your vehicle on the night of a full moon, a black 1964 pickup truck will appear and drive toward you at high speed. If you flee and the truck catches up to you, your vehicle will crash, resulting in fatalities. The origins of this legend are unknown.

- Mysterious wailing is not to be confused with the legend of the banshee, which follows. This legend says that wailing, sobbing, whimpering and other mysterious noises can be heard emanating from the church. I did not hear anything like this; if anything, I would describe the area as oddly quiet.

- According to legend, a banshee or group of banshees wailing caused congregants to abandon the church at one point in its history. Banshees originated in Ireland and Scotland, and there is no evidence that they ever migrated across the pond, but anything is possible. I just did not see or hear a banshee. Also, the church is active and holds regular services.

Is a banshee really to blame for the mysterious reports at Oakey Streak? *Wikimedia Commons.*

- There is a grave of someone who died on Friday the 13, times three. A headstone in the cemetery has this inscription "In Memory of Infant Triplet Sons of H.F. and M.L. Cain, Born Dec. 11. 1889, Died June 13, 1890." The mystery lies in the cause of their deaths: how did the three infants die on the same day? My research has not uncovered the answer.

- The cemetery contains the graves of numerous slaves, who are memorialized by a large monument erected in modern times. Are slaves among those haunting the grounds? Legends don't say.

- Hellhounds are rumored to roam the cemetery at night. If the site of their glowing red eyes is not enough to frighten passersby, the hellhounds will give chase and run trespassers off the grounds. I was unable to test this theory because I visited in the daytime, but it seems difficult to believe.

- Mysterious footsteps when no one is around are just another haunting rumor than can be applied to any haunted location. While I think that I did hear something, I will never know if that was just my imagination or not.

- Rumors of a haunting that could lead to your death align with the little ghost boy said to appear in the cemetery. If the spectral boy rolls you a ball and you pick it up and give it back to him or roll it back to him, you will die. I experienced neither the ghost boy or his ball, but if I had, I doubt I would have tested the veracity of the legend by rolling the ball back.

- There are numerous unmarked graves in Oakey Streak, including a section for babies. A simple marker says that twenty-one unknown infants are buried in one plot.

A marker noting the area of twenty-one unmarked infant graves. *Author's collection.*

- Supposedly, if you enter an old outhouse that still stands behind the church, spectral forces will keep you from opening the door, trapping you inside. There was no outhouse on the grounds at the time of my visit. This tale is probably taken from the nearby Constellation Church Cemetery. Many ghostly tales are often confused between the two different locations.

All of the legends of the hauntings seem to be oral and/or internet legend with little to no real documentation of any paranormal activity. So, it should be easy just to write the entire legend off to that of just hearsay. But why are so many legends, a mishmash of oral and internet tales, centered on this place? And how do I explain my own visceral reactions to the site? Like all legends, this one is left for the reader to decide.

If you decide to investigate for yourself, please know that it is located on private property; local law enforcement officers are aware of the legends and patrol the area frequently.

7

CHURCH STREET CEMETERY AND THE HAUNTED BOYINGTON OAK

When looking for haunted places in Alabama, one of the first on the list is the Church Street Cemetery, also known as the Church Street Graveyard, in downtown Mobile. Several spirits reportedly frequent this cemetery, but none is more well-liked and revered than that of Joe Cain—the man who revived Alabama's Mardi Gras following the Civil War.

Anytime you visit his final resting place, you will likely find it covered in colorful beads or other Mardi Gras decorations that devoted followers have left for afterlife celebrations.

Cain was a Confederate veteran of the War Between the States who returned home to find Mobile in a somber state. In hopes of brightening the blighted city and bringing some joy to residents, as well as spiting Union control over the city, Cain decided to revitalize a lost French tradition of celebrating Mardi Gras, which began in Mobile in 1701—before the New Orleans celebrations—but was suspended during the war.

In 1866, Cain—dressed as a Chickasaw Indian—led a group of revelers up and down Government Street. Cain's ragtag band grew into the celebration we know today. In Mobile, the Sunday before Fat Tuesday is celebrated as Joe Cain Day. It is not the least bit surprising that to this day, people report seeing the apparition of Joe parading through one of Mobile's oldest cemeteries.

Church Street Graveyard was established in 1819 by the City of Mobile for yellow fever victims. The first burials in the cemetery were those of early French and Spanish settlers and American pioneers. Even though the

The Church Street Cemetery seems peaceful on a sunny day. *Author's collection.*

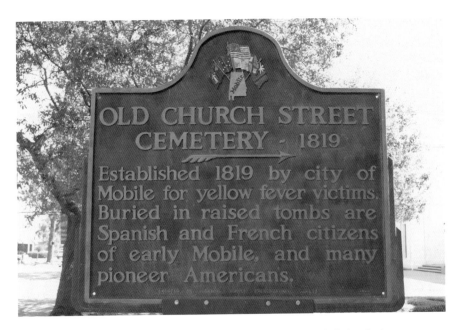

The historical marker at the Church Street Cemetery in Mobile. *Author's collection.*

cemetery now lies in downtown Mobile, it was more than half a mile from the city when it was founded. The cemetery was open and accepted burials until 1898, when it was officially closed, although the occasional burial has occurred since then with special permission from the city council.

In addition to the ghost of Joe Cain, the ghost of a small child is rumored to play among the tombstones in search of someone who might like to join. But the most well-known spirit haunting the cemetery is that of Charles Boyington.

The most common telling of this legend says that Charles Boyington was a printer who came to Mobile from Connecticut in 1833. Charles was known to be a vagabond who also had a gambling problem. Shortly after his arrival, he was befriended by a local introverted man named Nathaniel Frost. The two became fast friends and would often spend their afternoons in the calming confines of the Church Street Graveyard.

In May 1834, Boyington and Frost were seen together walking near the cemetery, and the next morning, Frost's body was discovered on the grounds, covered with stab wounds. Boyington was the first and only suspect in the crime. When authorities went looking for him, he had left town. He was soon apprehended and charged with the murder, although he proclaimed his innocence. He was found guilty of the murder, and in February 1835, he was marched through the streets of Mobile behind a wagon carrying a casket that would soon be his. Up until the noose was slipped on his neck, Boyington continued to deny having anything to do with the crime and proclaimed a mighty oak tree would sprout forth from his heart and grow atop his grave as proof of his innocence. A year after his death, a live oak grew from Boyington's grave. People who pass the site at night claim Charles can be heard whispering from the tree.

Another version of the story says that Charles was persecuted because he was a black man. He was found guilty with little to no evidence before being put to death.

Another story says that Charles was not a vagabond or gambler. He had simply become focused on a local woman, which caused him to lose focus on his job and get fired. When his friend Nathaniel offered to help him with his bills, Charles became enraged and killed him. Yet another version says that Charles killed Nathanial to steal a stash of money Nathaniel had saved.

Legends also give differing locations for Boyington's grave. Some accounts say the grave was initially located in a potter's field inside the cemetery walls, but the walls were moved after hurricane damage some years later, placing the tree and grave site outside the wall. Others say he

The cursed Boyington Oak sits outside the wall of the Church Street Cemetery. *Author's collection.*

had to be buried outside the wall because murderers could not be interred in consecrated ground.

Either way, the tree known today as the Boyington Oak is located just a few feet outside of the Church Street Cemetery wall. Murder victim Nathaniel Frost is reportedly buried in the graveyard near the place where he took his final breaths.

The true story is quite similar to the legend. Boyington was a white man who relocated to Mobile from Connecticut in 1833. He lived in a local boardinghouse, where he met and became friends with Nathaniel Frost. Some records say he was eventually fired from his job for lack of productivity due to daydreaming. Frost was killed shortly after Boyington's firing, seemingly giving Charles motive to steal from his friend. Adding to the appearance of guilt is the fact that Charles did leave town when officers went searching for him.

A May 1934 article in a Mobile newspaper offered a reward of $250 for Boyington's arrest. Soon after, Boyington was found aboard the river ship *James Monroe* en route to Montgomery, where he was arrested. After Boyington's arrest and incarceration, a local priest named William Hamilton took interest in Boyington and spent days trying to convince him to confess to the murder and convert to Christianity. Charles did neither.

On the day of his execution, the real Boyington did walk behind a wagon carrying his casket, and he did make a speech proclaiming his innocence after attempting to flee from the gallows and again being captured. During his speech, Boyington moved around the platform, avoiding execution, until the executioner pushed him from the structure to carry out the sentence. It is also true that an oak tree grew from Boyington's grave, although there is no evidence of a headstone, if there ever was one. The tree at the site thought to be his grave is frequently visited by those who have heard the legend.

Today, Church Street Graveyard is in need of maintenance. Many stones are deteriorating or broken. But the headstones of historical interest, including those of early Jewish residents etched in Hebrew, make it a must-see when visiting Mobile. If you go, be sure to visit the grave of Edmund P. Gaines, the man who arrested Aaron Burr for treason in Wakefield, Alabama.

8

HUNTSVILLE'S
DEAD CHILDREN'S PLAYGROUND

It looks like an ordinary playground—a set of swings, a teeter-totter, a slide—but at night, this place of play evokes a feeling of foreboding. Is there a presence, or was it the swings moving with the breeze? Could the playground really be haunted, or have rumors led imaginations to run wild?

If you have ever contemplated a visit to Huntsville in the north-central part of the state and did some online research, you likely stumbled upon tales of a legendary playground located in a cemetery. It is Huntsville's claim to paranormal fame, locally referred to as the Dead Children's Playground, because what could be more terrifying than a playground filled with ghost children? Don't worry, though; it is not actually located on cemetery grounds. That would be a little too creepy. The Dead Children's Playground, real name Maple Hill Park, rests in a small cove just outside the walls of historic Maple Hill Cemetery.

The playground is set in an indentation below a roadway and surrounded by natural rock walls and trees, forming a dark cove. It is easy to see how the park could live up to its haunted reputation. The legend behind the hauntings dates back one hundred years, claiming children buried in the adjoining cemetery eternally play there. It is said that these ghostly children are the spirits of those who perished in the 1918–19 Spanish flu epidemic.

As World War I was winding down, a pandemic like the world had never seen was making its way from country to country, killing an estimated twenty to fifty million people. The outbreak started in Spain, leading to the name

The Dead Children's Playground has long been known as Huntsville's most haunted location. *Author's collection.*

of the epidemic. It soon made its way to the United States, first in Kansas, and then in Alabama, where Huntsville was ground zero for the outbreak. In October 1918, Dr. Walker Booker England Sr. diagnosed the first local patient with the flu. The patient's brother, a soldier, had just come to visit, and doctors felt he had brought the disease to the area. Patient zero had been out the previous day selling beef in the Lincoln Village area of Huntsville, which helped the contagion spread through town like wildfire. Dr. England died from the flu on October 12, 1918.

Dr. Carl Grote, the county health officer, had been called to assist in the initial diagnosis and would play an important part in helping Madison County get through the outbreak, especially considering many physicians and pharmacists died fighting the flu. Things became so bad in Huntsville that the city was placed under a curfew. Dr. Grote's son Carl Jr. would later recount his father telling stories of the severity of the outbreak, saying, "You would catch it in the morning and be dead by night." Many of those affected were children, who were more susceptible to catching the disease and less likely to be able to fight it once they did.

Many parents lost numerous children to the outbreak, and tiny coffins were made in record numbers. Most of the children were buried in Maple Hill

Masked nurses stand ready with stretchers during the Spanish flu outbreak in 1918. *Library of Congress.*

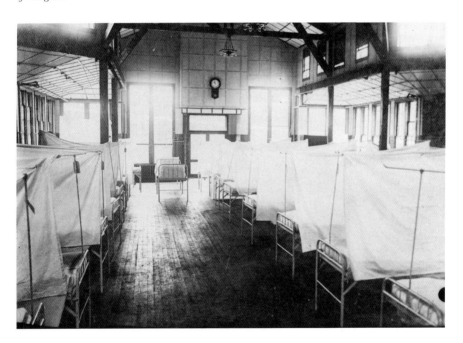

Interior of Red Cross House during the influenza epidemic. The beds are isolated by curtains. *Library of Congress.*

Cemetery, Huntsville's oldest cemetery and the official municipal burying ground that included a potter's field, or resting place for the indigent. It was on the grounds of the beautiful, park-like cemetery that parents wept over the graves of their children, grieving amid the freshly turned graves prepared for the next wave of bodies. It is the children buried there during the epidemic who are said to visit the playground next door, where they continue to seek children's pastimes, even after death.

One other story gives an explanation for the ghost children at Maple Hill Park, but this story has much less substantiation. The legend says that in the mid- to late 1950s, a killer abducted three children in the Chapman Mountain area of Huntsville, killing two of them. The killer is said to have buried their bodies on the hill overlooking the playground. The third kidnapped child supposedly escaped and turned the man in to the police. Some say the spirits of the two dead children haunt the playground, as their souls could not rest after being murdered.

Witnesses report hearing the sounds of children playing at night when no one is there and seeing the swings move by themselves as if propelled by a person. Many a Huntsville native has a story about an experience in the Dead Children's Playground, and visitors with an interest in the paranormal

Marker for the potter's field at Maple Hill Cemetery. Many of these people were lost during the Spanish flu outbreak. *Author's collection.*

After burying someone in the potter's field, families would save money to later put a headstone on their loved one's grave. *Author's collection.*

are always keen to visit the site. It not uncommon to visit the park and find graffiti that is satanic in nature, related to voodoo and witches' spells or the summoning of the dead. Several area residents are convinced that a coven of witches routinely visits the park at night to practice its craft.

It is also a rite of passage among teens in the Tennessee Valley to visit the playground at night to prove their bravery. This has led to other teens trying to frighten their friends by tying fishing line to the swings and to make them move or hiding audio players in the bushes with recorded sounds of children playing. All, of course, leading to a good scare for those brave enough to visit and adding fuel to the legends surrounding the park.

In the late 1990s and early 2000s, increased crime in the park made it unsafe to visit. Huntsville's mayor decided to have the playground equipment removed in hopes of preventing further activity. When the playground equipment was unexpectedly removed, city residents expressed outrage and began a campaign, which not only saved the park but resulted in the installation of new playground equipment as well. Yet even with the new playground equipment, rumors of the hauntings persist.

Maple Hill Park is not the only Huntsville location where hauntings connected to the Spanish flu have been reported. Not far away in downtown

Huntsville lies Walker Avenue, a quiet, residential street. Legend says children who died from the flu can be heard playing in the street, sometimes singing a song from the era:

> *I had a bird*
> *And its name was Inza*
> *I opened up the window*
> *And in flew Inza.*

This was a song parents taught their children to remind them to keep windows shut so influenza would not get inside the house. While not as well known as the hauntings at the Dead Children's Playground, the Walker Avenue haunting is made creepier by the song from the deadly epidemic.

Those who decide to visit the Dead Children's Playground should keep in mind the park closes at sunset. Due to the popularity of the legends surrounding the park, officers from the Huntsville Police Department frequently patrol the area, especially at night and during the Halloween season.

9

FISH THE SIZE OF VOLKSWAGENS

Legends of monster fish have their beginnings in yarns told by fishermen of oversized fish or the fish that got away. They aren't unique to Alabama, of course; some tales are set in well-known local fishing spots. You've likely heard a story like this one found online:

> Have you heard about the catfish down by Guntersville Dam? They sit on the bottom near the water intake for the turbines, and they just have all the food they could want float by their mouths. They get big as Volkswagens. There was a Tennessee Valley Authority diver a couple of years ago, he was down checking the intakes, doing their yearly inspection, when he saw the eyes come up, like they were rising out of the river bottom, and they were gigantic. He was scared out of his mind, and he didn't even know what he was seeing. It wasn't till he was racing back to the surface that he looked down, and he saw that it was a giant catfish that had been giving him the stare-down. He swore that it was the size of a small car. We always knew them giant catfish were down there. They were in the river before the dam was built, and after the dam, they just get bigger and bigger.

There are other versions across the internet, including this cautionary tale:

> My friend's uncle was a fisherman down on the river near Lake Wheeler, and he used to warn us about the man-eaters that were out in the water. He said there were some Blue Cats down there he'd seen that were four hundred

or five hundred pounds. They mostly only swim at night so they have better chance of sneaking up on something. He would say, "You better be careful if you go out on the river at night, if you fall in the water you gonna be fish food. One of them big cats gonna take you down to bottom and drown you and eat you a little bit at a time, and you wouldn't be the first."

If you haven't heard that one either, try this one:

It was about 1970, and my grandfather was running some trot lines out in the Alabama River one day. He put them out the night before, and he went back to pull them in and get the fish off, except there weren't any fish on the line, just a bunch of empty hooks. Then the line got tight and wouldn't come up, and he figured it got caught in a boat wake and snagged something under the water. He was just about to cut the line when it started pulling. Old Pappy thought he had him a big one on the line, so he starts pulling that line and fighting it with all he had. Then one of his buddies who had finished his fishing for the night saw Pappy and went over to help. Both men pulled and pulled for more than an hour trying to find out what was on that line. Then just like that, the granddaddy of all Flatheads popped up to the surface all wrapped up in that trot line. It seems he had just been eating all the little fish my grandfather had on the line and got himself all wrapped up, and while fighting with the two men, he got more tangled and tired. Now the two old fishermen knew he was an old Flathead 'cause of his size. He was so big they would swamp the boat just trying to pull him in. So they decided out of respect for his age to just cut him loose and let him out of this predicament. My grandfather told me several times that just after sunset he would sometimes see the old Flathead out in the middle of the river just like an old friend. As far as I know, no one else ever saw or caught him to this day. He is probably still out there.

You've likely heard at least one version of a similar tale. Stories of giant fish have been around since the days of Jonah being swallowed by the whale. Here in Alabama, these tales have been around for one hundred or more years, growing larger in scope in the 1940s, when dams starting popping up on Alabama rivers. As the stories grew, so did the fish.

What started out in the 1800s as fish that were the size of men have grown through the ages to now be the size of cars. The Volkswagen Beetle seems to be the standard by which current giant catfish are judged. Almost every river in the state has legends of giant fish. In both Guntersville Dam and

A dangerous waters sign on the Tennessee River above Guntersville Dam, the rumored home to giant catfish. *Author's collection.*

Wilson Dam along the Tennessee River, numerous stories abound about the Volkswagen-sized catfish that live below the dam, but no one has ever produced one or even a photo of one.

It is true that the largest species of catfish in North America is the blue catfish, which resides in Alabama waters. However, they can't reach the sizes described in legends. The current world record–holding blue cat weighed a whopping 143 pounds and was caught in North Carolina. Several other blue cats caught throughout the South have gone over the 100-pound mark.

Flathead catfish is another large breed of catfish native to Alabama, but once again, they do not get anywhere near the size of the stories that surround them.

As a helpful guide for those who might go out to the river, here are some of North America's largest freshwater species, the real fish behind the legends:

PADDLEFISH can grow up to five feet long and weigh up to sixty pounds. They get their name from their paddle-shaped snouts, which they use to dig in the ground in search of vegetation to eat.

BULL SHARKS can live in saltwater and in bodies of fresh water connecting to the ocean. In the Mississippi River, they have been found as far north as Cairo, Illinois, and there have been a few caught in Alabama's Lake

Do giant catfish lurk in these waters around Guntersville Dam? *Author's collection.*

A monster sunfish caught by W.N. McMillan on April 1, 1910. The estimated weight was 3,500 pounds. This is not a freshwater fish but still giant. *Library of Congress.*

Guntersville in the last few years. These sharks can reach eleven and a half feet in length and can weigh more than five hundred pounds, and yes, they are aggressive. Numerous reports detail unprovoked attacks on humans.

ALLIGATOR GAR is a nasty-looking fish that has a toothy mouth resembling that of an alligator. This large freshwater fish has a long snout and two rows of fang-like teeth that make it look particularly vicious. These fish can reach ten feet in length and weigh up to 350 pounds.

WHITE STURGEON are easily the largest freshwater fish in North America. They can reach twenty feet in length and weigh up to 1,500 pounds. These large fish can live in fresh or salt water and can be found in the western United States and Canada.

As with the legend of Bigfoot, lack of evidence doesn't mean monster river fish aren't real. When I was growing up in Guntersville, I heard tales of a giant catfish that lived by the dam. One story says that in the 1990s, when builders were erecting a new river bridge, blasting of underwater pylons stunned some two-hundred-pound catfish that floated to the surface. Several people witnessed the huge fish on the water but couldn't get photos before state officials removed them. That's how the story goes, at least.

10

THE TALE OF THE COOSA RIVER MONSTER

Have you ever heard of the Coosa River Monster, an Alabama version of the Loch Ness Monster? Amazingly, tales of river monsters continue even today, when the existence of such serpents has largely been debunked. People continue to be fascinated by legends of creatures such as Champ in the Great Lakes or Nessie in Scotland.

Today, many legends are centered on tales of "Catzilla" or giant catfish that call the rivers home, but before these ruled our imagination, tales of serpents were commonplace. The most prevalent of Alabama's river monster legends is the Coosa River Monster, which was last reported in the mid-1800s but whose specter remains. In June 1877, the *Gadsden Times* reported the "Sea Monster of the Coosa" was sighted by Marcus L. Foster, a local man who had been setting up trot lines near the community of Ball Play.

The article states Foster was setting out the lines near the mouth of the creek when his attention was diverted to what looked like a man standing in a slow-moving boat on the opposite bank. Foster decided to approach the other fisherman and crossed the river. As he drew closer, the figure seemed to change to that of a woman standing in the water, with half of her body visible above the surface. When he was within fifty yards of the woman, he realized he wasn't seeing a human at all but some type of serpentine monster.

Foster reported a head and neck resembling those of a horse ascending from the water. It had large, bulging eyes, and a fiery red tongue was visible in its open mouth. Foster was understandably unnerved by the sight and paddled back to the bank while watching the monster float

Right: A political cartoon of a sea serpent in 1895 reveals that people believed in them even then. *Library of Congress*.

Below: A drawing of steamboat travel on Alabama waterways circa 1831. *Library of Congress*.

quietly along before submerging. Three people reported witnessing the sea monster in 1877.

But there were sightings even before then. The Coosa River Monster legend was allegedly first documented in an 1816 letter stating that a number of Saint Clair County settlers near Ten Islands had killed a sea monster that was sick and found half on shore and half in the water. When the belly of the beast was sliced open, intact remains of a "recently eaten Indian, his canoe, a deer, a bow with arrows and a rifle" were found inside, reports claim. Everyone believed the creature had become ill from the metal in the rifle.

Reports began again in 1862 when a woman whose last name was Martin and a local judge named Lemuel Standifer reported seeing a serpentine head breaking the water on different occasions. Esteemed riverboat captain J.M. Elliott also reported seeing a mysterious leviathan drifting along the Coosa approaching Rome, Georgia. Some retellings of this account state that Judge Standifer was with Captain Elliott when this encounter was known to have happened.

Reports of a river monster spanning a period of several years were enough to drive parents and local news media to warn children against playing on the banks of the river lest they become monster food. Even as stories of the river monster dwindled, speculation continued to run high about a creature. Then, in 1882, an intrepid reporter set out on the Coosa River in a rowboat to document the monster. After several tedious hours, "a commotion commenced near the eastern bank about a mile and a half above the Broad Street wharf," his account said. The reporter encountered a huge black mass swirling beneath the water's surface and rising from the depths. "The sight," he reported, "was a thrilling one and well-calculated to alarm anyone." But closer examination showed the sea monster was only "a great mass of leaves and weeds" brought up from the bottom of the river by the gasses and currents.

For the most part, rumors of the river monster quieted after this, even though the legends were never completely forgotten and are retold to this day.

One possible explanation for the sightings dates back to the 1830s. In 1834, while reports of river monsters were still prevalent, fossils of giant lizard-like creatures, *Basilosaurus cetoides*, were found in Alabama near the Gulf of Mexico and later in more northern counties such as Choctaw, Clarke and Washington. Paleontologists later declared these fossils to be that of a prehistoric meat-eating whale that grew as long as seventy feet, known as zeuglodon.

Basilosaurus cetoides was later declared the state fossil of Alabama. It is unknown whether a few of these whales managed to survive into the Coosa River in the 1800s, spurring legends of river monsters. In any case, the description of the zeuglodon head does not seem to match those of the river serpent.

Another possible candidate behind the sightings is the alligator gar, a fish that dates back to the time when dinosaurs roamed North America. Their heavy bodies and bony structure make them good candidates for consideration as the river monster, although gar have long bone appendages as noses, which do not fit the serpents' descriptions. Perhaps there truly are river horses roaming Alabama's waterways that go unreported by witnesses because they think no one would believe them.

11

THE LEGEND OF LONNIE STEPHENS, THE VANISHING HITCHHIKER

Here is how one man described his encounter with the legendary vanishing hitchhiker of north Alabama:

It was a stormy summer night and I was easing my truck through the driving rain on the outskirts of Decatur. The water falling from the heavens was so heavy and the fog so thick that I was doing good to make ten miles per hour while looking for a place to pull off the road and wait out the small monsoon. It was then that I spotted the young man walking along the edge of the roadway. I hesitated. After all, everyone knows the dangers of stopping for strangers on the side of the road, but this night was truly not meant for man or beast to be outdoors. I edged my four-wheel drive to the shoulder of the road behind the young man. As I watched him, he suddenly disappeared. Vanished right before my eyes.

It isn't every day a fully formed young man walking along the road vanishes, and watching it happen was unnerving. To ensure the lad had not fallen or crouched beside the truck, I got out to check. Nothing. The rain was still coming down in sheets, so I climbed back in the truck to wait for a lull and tried to convince myself there had never been a hitchhiker, that the rain had created an illusion. In that endeavor, I was unsuccessful. I decided I'd research the area when I had a chance and try to find out who the man could have been.

It seemed I was not the first person to have an encounter with a vanishing figure on that particular stretch of road. I discovered several reports, as well as a short history on the mysterious ghostly walker. His name is recorded as Lonnie Stephens, and he has been appearing to drivers on Limestone County Road 117 since the early 1940s.

This is his tale: Lonnie Stephens was falsely accused of murdering his girlfriend in September 1934, and it was not until many years later that the real killer confessed. But it was too late for Lonnie. The innocent man managed to escape from a chain gang and was attempting to hitch a ride when he was struck and killed by a car. And that's why Lonnie's ghost can still be seen walking along that stretch of road, his hand outstretched in an imploring gesture.

The example above has all the elements of a great ghost story: lost love, a wrongly accused man and his tragic death just before his innocence could be proclaimed. It seems like a good story because that's just what it is. There was no Lonnie Stephens accused of murder in 1934 in north Alabama, nor is there a record of Lonnie Stephens being killed in a car accident in any of the following years.

Lonnie's tale is just one of many urban legends of ghostly hitchhikers that persist throughout the world and even predate the automobile. There are so many that it would be impossible to list them all, but for the most part, the hitchhiker legends fit into seven categories.

VERSION 1: A driver picks up a hitchhiker who wants to be taken to a particular address. When the driver arrives at the address, the hitchhiker has mysteriously disappeared from the vehicle. When inquiring at the address, the driver learns that the hitchhiker was the ghost of a person who once lived in the home or had some tie to the address. Stories with this theme can be found in at least sixteen states in the United States.

VERSION 2: A driver picks up a hitchhiker who proceeds to prophesy an impending disaster. When the driver turns to find the hitchhiker gone, he asks around and learns the hitchhiker had been the spirit of a dead man. The dire messages are warnings to the drivers. These types of stories are circulated worldwide.

VERSION 3: A young man meets a young lady at a public place, and he asks her to join him for a ride in his car. In their discussions, she tells him she lives on the opposite side of town and gives the street address. Chilly, the young lady borrows the man's jacket and forgets to give it back to him at the end of the night when he returns her to the place they met. The next day, when the man goes to the woman's address to retrieve the item, he finds the address is a cemetery. He walks through the grounds and sees his jacket, lying atop a grave marked with the girl's name. Stories such as these can be found in many countries and all fifty states.

VERSION 4: A driver picks up a hitchhiker and takes him to a given address. The driver later discovers that the hitchhiker left something in the car and goes back to the address to return the item. The person who answers the door admits the hitchhiker once lived there but says he is dead. The item left behind is identified as belonging to the dead person.

VERSION 5: A driver sees a hitchhiker and stops to pick him up, but the hitchhiker suddenly vanishes before getting into the car. When the driver relates his story, he learns a person matching the hitchhiker's description was killed in that spot some years earlier. This story fits the Lonnie Stephens legend.

VERSION 6: A driver picks up a hitchhiker, offering to take him to his requested destination. During the ride, the driver recounts the story of a deadly wreck caused by a reckless driver on that stretch of road and admonishes the hitchhiker to avoid similar dangers by being a vigilant driver. At his destination, the hitchhiker exits the car and goes into a diner, where he mentions the man's tale. That's when he learns the driver was the man killed in the crash and the hitchhiker had been traveling with a ghost.

VERSION 7: A driver picks up a melancholy hitchhiker who says he is troubled because he is recalling a death that occurred on the road on the same day years earlier. After dropping off the hitchhiker, the driver learns he had given a ride to the ghost of the person who was killed and who returns to the site each year on the anniversary of his death.

These are cautionary tales, reminders that you never know who is getting in your car when you stop to pick up a stranger. They are meant to make you think twice when you see a shadowy figure walking along the edge of a dark, secluded road.

Did You Know

David Allan Coe's song "The Ride" is a modern telling of the hitchhiker legend in which a man catches a ride with the ghost of music legend and Alabama native Hank Williams. The song ends with the line "This is where you get off, boy, 'cause I'm goin' back to Alabam."

12

THE STRANGE DISAPPEARANCE OF ORION WILLIAMSON

Orion Williamson lived a quiet, unassuming life with his wife and son on a small farm near Selma, Alabama—until a July day in 1854. According to local legend, one particularly hot afternoon, Orion went out of his farmhouse to move his horses to a more shaded area of pasture to offer them some protection from the harsh sun. His wife would later say that after he stepped off the porch, Orion picked up a small stick, which he absentmindedly swished back and forth as he walked through the ankle-high grass. With his trek into the pasture halfway completed, Orion lifted a foot and simply vanished in mid-stride as his wife and son watched. His wife, fearing the worst, jumped up and ran from the porch toward the spot where her husband had just been.

It turns out that she was not the only one who was shocked when Orion disappeared. Neighbors Armour Wren and his son were returning from Selma on a road that ran by Williamson's farm. The pair saw Williamson walking toward them through the field so they stopped the buggy to greet their neighbor. But they never got the chance; according to Wren, right after Orion waved at them, he simply disappeared. This, of course, alarmed them, and they jumped off the buggy to run to the spot of his disappearance.

Mrs. Williamson and the Wrens reached the spot where they had seen Orion disappear and found no trace of the farmer. They also noticed the ground where he last stood was now barren and devoid of grass. One moment, Orion Williamson had been walking away from his family and waving at friends—and the next moment, he had vanished into thin air.

Orion Williamson supposedly disappeared while plowing a field such as this near Selma. *Library of Congress*.

For more than two hours, the Wrens and the Williamsons searched the field. They found nothing, and suddenly struck with the realization of what had happened, Mrs. Williamson collapsed in shock. She was taken to Selma and hospitalized. When news spread of the incident, three hundred men from town gathered at the field. They formed three hand-to-hand ranks and slowly inched their way across the grass, stopping every few feet to kneel and search for openings or holes. They searched the field dozens of times, and when night fell, they used torches and lanterns to light the area. Bloodhounds were brought in, but no trace of the farmer could be found.

The following morning, hundreds of other volunteers arrived from nearby communities, along with authorities and a team of geologists. To determine if the ground itself was solid, the searchers began digging at the point where Williamson disappeared, but a few feet below the surface, they hit solid bedrock. There were no cave-ins, crevices, quicksand or holes to explain where the farmer had gone. He had simply disappeared.

Though Selma was a small community, word of the disappearance quickly spread, bringing journalists from around the South and Midwest to investigate the mysterious tale.

Events seemed to get stranger. In the spring of 1855, when grass covered the fields, none would grow in the spot where Williamson was last seen, which mystified investigators who were still interested in the case. Mrs. Williamson, who was still so traumatized by the vanishing that she refused to speak of it, was of little help to the investigators. Instead, her strange behavior evoked curiosity.

Why was Mrs. Williamson still in such a state of shock after a year had gone by? True, the disappearance of her husband was undoubtedly bizarre, but why did she refuse to talk about him? Later, in 1855, she finally answered these questions and, in so doing, added to the mystery.

With a quavering voice, Mrs. Williamson revealed the rest of the story. She told the searchers that in the days following her husband's disappearance, she and her child distinctly heard Orion's voice calling for help from the spot where he had vanished. Each time they heard him, they ran to the spot, but there was no one and nothing there. The calls for help continued for almost two weeks, with Williamson's voice becoming weaker and weaker as the days passed. On the last night he was heard, the family slept outside on the edge of the vanishing spot. They heard Williamson's whispers and then he was heard no more.

As the story spread, a teenage boy in Ohio by the name of Ambrose Bierce came across it. The story helped instill a lifelong fascination with the unknown in the young man and inspired him to later investigate the story.

Ambrose Gwinnet Bierce would go on to be a soldier, editorialist, fabulist satirist and renowned short story writer, but for some time he worked as

Was Orion Williamson's voice really heard in the field well after his disappearance? *Library of Congress.*

a journalist at the *San Francisco Examiner*. It was during his time with this newspaper that he investigated Williamson's disappearance.

Bierce interviewed the searchers in the Williamson affair as well as experts who claimed to have theories as to where the farmer had gone. One of them, Dr. Maximilian Hern, was a scientist who had written a book called *Disappearance and Theory Thereof*. He stated that Williamson had walked into a "void spot of universal ether." These spots, he explained, only lasted for a few seconds but were capable of destroying any and all material elements that happened into them. Other scientists came forward with theories as well. One of them said that he believed Williamson walked into a periodic "magnetic field" that disintegrated his atomic structure and sent him into another dimension.

Bierce published "The Difficulty of Crossing a Field" in the *San Francisco Examiner* on October 14, 1888. He would go on to publish several short stories he claimed were inspired by the Williamson vanishing. Most famous of these were "The Spook House" and "Charles Ashmore's Trail," the latter of which is about a young boy who disappeared while fetching water outside his family's house.

From the content of Bierce's works, it becomes obvious that he was obsessed with the unknown. He made a name for himself by writing about it. One has to wonder if, while writing his fantastical stories, he had a premonition that he would meet the same fate as so many of his characters.

In December 1913, a then seventy-one-year-old Bierce told people he wanted to travel to Mexico and ride with Pancho Villa during the Mexican Revolution. He apparently reached his destination. In a letter to his niece Lora, Bierce wrote: "If you hear of my being stood up against a Mexican stone wall and shot to rags please know that I think that is a pretty good way to depart this life. It beats old age, disease, or falling down the cellar stairs. To be a gringo in Mexico—ah, that is euthanasia."

Just before Bierce entered war-torn Mexico, he again wrote Lora, "I shall not be here long enough to hear from you, and don't know where I shall be next. Guess it doesn't matter much. Adios, Ambrose."

Lora received one more letter, in which Bierce said he "expected to leave the next day, partly by rail, for Okinawa, where Villa was poised to attack a cornered federal army." This last letter was dated December 26, 1913, and postmarked Chihuahua, Mexico. It is the last known correspondence from Ambrose Bierce, who was never heard from again. His disappearance is a mystery to this day, much like that of Selma farmer Orion Williamson, which first captured a young Bierce's attention.

13

WOLF WOMAN OF MOBILE

Imagine, if you will, walking along a quiet, residential street on a cool April evening with the salt air gently blowing from the bay. As you round a curve, you are unprepared for what you see—just as you are unprepared to explain it. You know that what you are seeing couldn't, or *shouldn't*, be real. Not here in one of Alabama's largest cities. Standing just a stone's throw away is a creature that appears to have the lower half of a wolf or dog but the top half of a woman. It is walking on four legs, which also doesn't seem right. You really aren't sure how to feel about what you see—other than frightened—but you feel you should warn others.

This scenario describes what occurred in the city of Mobile in 1971. On April 8, the *Mobile Press-Register* published a hand-drawn rendering of a half-woman, half-wolf headlined with the words "…But Would You Believe???"

The paper reported that during the previous week, the newspaper's office had received more than fifty phone calls reporting fearful sightings of the wolf woman. One early caller reported the creature "a woman and a wolf, pretty and hairy," which seemed to fit many of the descriptions coming in.

Soon the reports plunged some neighborhoods into panic. One unflappable teen told reporters with a straight face that he wouldn't venture into the streets at night. One unnamed local youth told the paper, "My Daddy sighted it down in a marsh, and it chased him home. Now, my Mommy keeps all the doors and windows locked."

The newspaper was not the only office getting calls—the police department was swarmed with reports. Sightings of the beast and reports

An artist's rendering of the Wolf Woman of Mobile that ran in the *Mobile Press Register*. *Author's collection.*

of it chasing or stalking people and animals were so rampant that the Mobile police opened an investigation into the matter. They feared that it was likely an animal stalking residents rather than some mythical creature. The reports and investigation centered along Davis Avenue and the Plateau area, where sightings of the monster were most often reported. While the police department never officially commented on the investigation, the unofficial story was that officers were never able to locate the creature or any physical evidence such as fur, paw prints or scat. A few days after the article's publication, reports ceased, the fear subsided, and the Wolf Woman of Mobile faded into obscure folklore.

Were the people of Mobile really subjected to a monster roaming their streets, or was something else at play?

It's likely the initial reports of the famed Wolf Woman were made on or around April 1. Was this an April Fool's prank gone awry, causing a mass panic in people? Was the newspaper staff in on the joke? With more than forty years having passed with no answers, it seems likely that we will never know the true story behind the mysterious Wolf Woman.

The question remains: Should we discount the possibility that these citizens really saw a mythical creature? The belief in werewolves is long held in European and Native American cultures. In European legends, people become werewolves unwillingly through a curse or by being bitten by someone already possessed of the curse.

In the Native American traditions, werewolves are more in tune with skin walkers, witches that can disguise themselves as animals for the purpose of

A *Mobile Press Register* newsboy circa 1920s. The legend of the Wolf Woman was spread through publication in the paper. *Library of Congress.*

harming someone. Legends say most skin walker magic is done with the sole intent to commit murder. Were the people of Mobile subject to a form of werewolf or skin walker that week in April? The answer is most probably no—the Wolf Woman never harmed anyone, according to reports.

Another option could explain the Wolf Woman sightings: a feral child who was taken by animals at a very young age and then raised among them so that it took on their mannerisms.

Rumors of feral children are common, leading to fictional tales like Tarzan. There are about forty reported cases of feral children who were raised by various animals, some of them even raised by wolves. When these children were found, they lacked the social skills necessary to fit into society and often were cast off by it.

While some cases are true, the legends of feral children throughout history are even more numerous. One making the rounds on the internet in modern times is the tale of the Lobo Wolf Girl of Devil's River, which dates back to 1945. More often than not, the tale is related as fact, although there is no evidence to support it.

So, does the Wolf Woman of Mobile fit into any of these categories? Technically, she fits all of them; in reality, she is probably just a good story to tell around the campfire, like any good urban legend.

14

THE PIEDMONT PUKWUDGIE

I f you have ever spent time in Alabama's glorious wilderness, you have undoubtedly come across something that is just a little on the unexplainable side. In college, when I would do a lot of hiking in and around the Talladega National Forest, rumors were rampant of a small, troll-like creature that roamed the woods. People soon named this mythical creature the Piedmont Pukwudgie, but no one seemed to know why.

The legend said if you looked directly at it, the pukwudgie would change to a woodland creature such as a porcupine or groundhog so as to go undetected. Old-timers would tell young people to be careful in the woods because the pukwudgie was known to lead hikers off a ledge to their deaths. Like most stories of strange tiny beings, this one tickled my imagination.

Tales of little people are common throughout the world in every culture. They include fairies, dwarves, gnomes, goblins, gremlins, brownies, trows, pygmies, abatwa and pukwudgies.

As much as I would have liked for these legendary creatures to turn out to be a leprechaun or perhaps a white-bearded gnome, those legends didn't originate in this area. The most likely to be found in Alabama would be the pukwudgie. According to many Native American legends, the pukwudgie are a race of little wild people that live in forests. They are noted to be human-like in appearance, between one and three feet tall, and have large noses and ears, with skin in various shades of gray. On the occasions they have reportedly been spotted, they have been described like the Hollywood version of a goblin or gnome.

Does a pukwudgie roam the forests near and around Piedmont? This picture taken from Bald Rock at Mount Cheaha shows a good view of the pukwudgie's terrain. *Author's collection.*

Many Indian tribes throughout North America such as Ojibwe, Algonquin, Abenaki, Mohican, Creek and Cherokee have legends about pukwudgies, though different tribal folklore ascribes different behaviors and powers exhibited by the creatures. They are variously described as:

- a mischievous but basically good-natured creature that plays tricks on people but is not dangerous
- dangerous and mean but only to people who disrespect, antagonize or harm them
- protectors of children who will remove them from abusive situations
- fickle, dangerous creatures who may play harmless tricks or even help a human neighbor but are just as likely to steal children or terrorize humans
- creatures that were once friendly with humans but turned against humanity after years of human disrespect
- evil creatures that will kill people to gain control of their souls
- having the ability to appear or disappear instantly and before your eyes

- having the ability to create magical fire with their hands to defend themselves if trapped
- forest spirits
- shape-shifters who can transform into animals when the need arises
- skilled weapon crafters who create knives and bows that shoot poisoned arrows

Tribes seem to agree, though, that puckwudgies should be left alone by humans. Researching this legend turned out to be much more difficult than I assumed. Yes, the internet is rife with tales of the little people, but that did me little good for finding out more about the Piedmont Pukwudgie or any pukwudgie specific to Alabama. In Calhoun County, I found few people who remembered tales of the Piedmont Pukwudgie that their grandparents warned them about. (It also didn't help that when researching the pukwudgie, my teenaged son asked what had me so enthralled. I showed him some illustrations of pukwudgies, and he said, "Dad, that's obviously a goblin.")

Then I read about a radio DJ named Luther Upton in the southwest town of Evergreen, the official Bigfoot Capital of Alabama, who recorded that a man from Pennsylvania called his radio station one morning to report that he had seen a pukwudgie standing by the side of Interstate 65 in Conecuh County.

When Upton spoke about the report on the radio, a listener in Flat Rock called to share sightings and rumors of pukwudgies in that community as well. Flat Rock is located in the same mountain chain as Piedmont, so it seemed a good place to continue my search, but I was unable to find any proof of pukwudgies or pukwudgie activity.

The internet did teach me that pukwudgie legends are more widespread than I realized. In the United States and Canada, there are reports of pukwudgie sightings from coast to coast. I didn't come across any reported sightings in Mexico, so I assume that south of the border, pukwudgie make easy prey to the infamous chupacabra, a.k.a. the Mexican Goat Killer. Websites devoted to unexplained hauntings are also filled with reports of the little forest people. Pukwudgie are so prevalent in American folklore that J.K. Rowling mentions them in her Harry Potter Universe franchise as the name of one of the wizarding houses in the American wizarding school Ilvermorny, the U.S. version of Hogwarts.

As I continued my research, I discovered my son was closer to the truth than I realized when he said the pukwudgie resembled a goblin. In the early parts of human history, nature was an exceedingly scary place. It is easy to see how cultures throughout the world used belief in creatures to explain things they did not yet understand. This seems to be particularly true of the Native Americans, who had such a bond with nature and would believe mischief or good luck could be attributed to creatures such as the pukwudgie. But I know without a doubt that those who have reported experiences with such beings are convinced of their existence. Perhaps the rest of us just need to catch up to their thinking.

15

BIGFOOT IN ALABAMA

The sun was low on the horizon and its light almost nonexistent as the car went around a sharp curve on the country road in rural Clay County. Just past the curve, the car's headlights shone on something by the side of the road. It was an oversized figure just at the edge of the tree line. Against his better judgment, the driver stopped the car and got out, not quite trusting his eyes. As the man watched, the tall creature turned toward him as if inspecting new prey. The man grew increasingly edgy as the creature looked him over, and the man's knees buckled when the huge creature yelled out, "Everything OK up there?"

The driver of the car, feeling a bit foolish, walked over to the now-apparent man standing in the field and said, "Goodness boy, you are so tall, I thought you were a Bigfoot."

While this encounter may seem a little outlandish, it is the true account of a recent Bigfoot sighting in Alabama, a state with a long history of alleged encounters. However, the stories seem to have become more prevalent with society's encroachment into wild areas, as well as the growing popularity of America's most notorious cryptid.

The Native Americans who settled the area we now refer to as Alabama had a fervent belief in the creature. Different native tribes called the creature *Eeyachuba*, *Yeahoh* or *Shampe*, just to name a few. Some common names used today are *Sasquatch*, *Yeti*, *Abominable Snow Man*, *Wooley Booger*, *Skunk Ape*, *Hairy Man* or sometimes just *Hairy Monster*.

In the early days of Alabama, communication between settlements was quite difficult, and people relied on travelers to hear news from other areas, so few Bigfoot sightings were recorded from those times. As time passed and travel became easier, information began to be recorded in letters and newspapers. Initially, only the larger communities had newspapers, so events that occurred in remote areas went unreported in the papers.

But Bigfoot made the headlines as early as 1894. On February 25, 1894, the *Constitution* in Atlanta, Georgia, had a report of "an unknown animal that was abroad in the area of Preston, Alabama. It was about the size of a two-year-old calf and very wide across the back. It is blackish of hue and makes a variety of strange noises. It is as wild as a deer and although many have seen the strange beast, nobody has ever gotten a shot at it."

In April 1936, several newspapers throughout the country reported a story from Anniston, Alabama. This version of the story is taken from the *Modesto Bee:*

> *On April 15, 1936 Sheriff W.P. Cotton dismissed a posse of "wild man" hunters and reported that an all-day search for a strange gorilla-like family in a Choccolocca Valley swamp was in vain. Cotton led a group of farmers and citizens into the swamp after rural residents reported seeing a man, woman and child whose bodies were covered with hair and at times walked on all fours.*

Alabama's diverse landscapes of dense woods, mountains, river valleys and flatlands would seem to make inviting habitats for a Bigfoot. And according to local lore, it is. Alabama history is filled with Bigfoot sightings, especially in Chilton, Conecuh, Tuscaloosa, Limestone and Morgan Counties. These counties represent only a small portion of sightings reported to the Bigfoot Field Research Organization (BFRO), a group dedicated to the study of sightings throughout the United States. Here are a few of the more detailed sightings:

In 1978, a fourteen-year-old saw a large creature, covered in blackish fur, wade into the Elk Creek approximately twelve miles from Athens. The creature did this twice, both times slapping the water as if trying to catch a fish. A similar creature, described as muscular, covered in black fur and about seven and a half feet tall, was reportedly seen in the Elk River area several times from 1993 through 1996. The most recent recorded sighting in Limestone County was in 2001, when a man reportedly saw an eight-foot-tall hairy creature cross the road in front of his vehicle in the Swan Creek

A Bigfoot display at Expedition Bigfoot in Georgia. *Author's collection.*

A Bigfoot "buttock imprint" at Expedition Bigfoot in Blue Ridge, Georgia. *Author's collection.*

Wildlife Management Area. There were also reports of people hearing strange howls during the night in the nearby Tanner area.

Two sightings in Morgan County in the year 2000 show just how close some people claim to have come to the elusive creature. In August of that year, three people were clearing land in the Brindlee Mountain area when they saw a large, reddish, manlike creature with no apparent neck standing a few hundred feet away in the shade of the tree line. A few months later in October, a husband and wife were riding the back roads of the Valhermoso Springs area looking for deer when they came upon "a large brown object that raised up straight on two legs, had long arms, broad shoulders and stood about seven to eight feet tall, and it was very hairy." The couple was about twenty yards from the creature. When it noticed them, it ran into the woods "with the speed of lightning." Reports of unknown wild animal noises from the woods persist throughout these areas to this day.

Madison County, one of the most populated counties in the state, would seem to be an area Bigfoot would avoid, yet there were several reported sightings from the 1940s through the 1990s. A 2009 sighting is by far the most interesting, because it takes place at the state's most visited destination.

On February 24, 2009, a guest who would like to remain anonymous was staying at the Marriott Hotel in Huntsville, adjacent to the U.S. Space & Rocket Center, which is the state's top tourist attraction. The guest, who until that time did not believe in the Bigfoot legend, was staying in room 614. As he stood on the balcony at about 5:45 a.m., he saw an unusual creature. He gave this description of the incident in his own words:

> I was staring off at the woods when something caught my eye. After focusing on it, I realized there were legs, then arms, then I could clearly make out his face. The creature stood six to seven feet tall and was staring directly back at me. It seemed to have fine hairs all over, gray-colored hair that got blacker as the hair got closer to the skin. The tips of the hair were much lighter—the face (lips, eye lids, etc.) were more of a very dark brown. It stood very erect, was very muscular, and did not seem to have the apelike protruding mouth and nose, but more flat faced and human like.
>
> After thirty seconds, he started rocking back and forth. I then realized it was moving and could in no way be mistaken for a deer or bear or anything else. It was a fully erect apelike animal that seemed to want me to see him. He rocked back and forth and from side to side. He continued to rock, then stood and stared at me. I was on the sixth floor, about 120 yards away, in decent lighting due to hotel lights and street light behind the loading area of the hotel.

He stared back but remained face forward with feet only about two feet apart. He leaned over to his left, and with his right arm, he started pulling bark off a very large pine tree; it looked as if someone were in a sawing position. After watching for about five minutes, I felt this creature was docile and smooth moving. I decided I would try and get a closer look. I ran out of the hotel room, and there was a security guard in our hall putting out the morning paper at the hotel room doors. I asked him to come with me. We ran around the corner outside, and as we were running, I finally got the nerve to tell him what I saw. We get to the reference points I had chosen, and there was a lot of fresh bark removed from the large pine tree. I tried to pull bark from it to no avail, it was too hard. I am six-foot, four and weigh three hundred pounds. I went back after 7:00 a.m. (light) and noticed what looked like scat. I put a handful in a Marriott laundry plastic bag.

One of the Marriott employees saw two large footprints, more like deep indentions in the pinestraw. I took off my shoe and placed my foot in it, and there was about a one-inch area all the way around my foot. Something very heavy had to make these indentions. I am 100 percent positive of the above description—I watched this clearly for five to six minutes!

In June 2005, a group of six friends camping on a clear night in Cheaha State Park in Talladega County had an up-close-and-personal experience with what they fully believed was a Bigfoot.

Every year me and a group of my friends camp in Cheaha State Park. Year before last, we were sitting outside our tent around the campfire, and it was about 11:00 at night. We where the ONLY ones in that camp site, so it was very quiet. We started to hear strange low noises, almost like an old chainsaw trying to crank. Following that was a very high-pitch humming noise. The sound was getting closer and closer. We took out our spotlight and scanned the woods. What we saw was very disturbing....It appeared to be an upright figure that was hairy and had a gray tint to its fur. It was standing behind a tree and was slightly hunching over, like it was hiding from us. We could see its back bowing out of the right side of the tree and its head coming out of the left. There's no doubt in my mind that it was an ape-like creature. It stood still for about thirty to sixty seconds. Then we decided to take the light off of it, to maybe see if it would move....About ten seconds later we turned the light back on and it was gone! The next night we heard two separate creatures but neither showed up.

It seems Bigfoot doesn't take time off for holidays; one Colbert County hunter reported an incident on Thanksgiving night just after dark while hunting near Alabama's famed Coon Dog Cemetery.

I was deer hunting in Freedom Hills Management Area around Coon Dog Cemetery. I entered the woods before daylight and walked down the access road next to a pine forest. I came to the back of some pines where they turned into heavy hardwoods. I sat down at the bottom of a tree and waited for daylight. During my way up, behind me on top of the ridge I heard a series of grunting and heavy movement through the woods walking down the ridge behind and down the ridge it went. Once daylight came, I walked up to where I first heard the grunting and movement. As I got to the area, I found bedding and hair. The hair I found I kept a sample, and it wasn't wild hog or bear nor mountain lion. This whole incident scared me and made me very uneasy. Later that night, we heard wood knocks and a tree pushed down.

The BFRO keeps the identities of most witnesses anonymous, and after reading some of their reported tales, you can see why. In today's world, the general consensus is that everything can be explained, and a story like any of these would be considered pure nonsense, spoken by a crazy person. This is why so many sightings go unreported.

With that in mind, revisit the beginning of this story. Put yourself in the car on the desolate road in the middle of nowhere. As you slowly round the

Purported Sasquatch hair on display at the Expedition Bigfoot Museum in Blue Ridge, Georgia. *Author's collection.*

Bigfoot claw marks on a tree near Evergreen as determined by Bigfoot hunters. *Courtesy of Lee Peacock.*

curve and see the outline of a large creature, the stories of the wild man your grandpa once told might flash through your mind. Your car gets closer to the creature, and it begins to run off with a stride much too long for a man. You look around and find yourself alone, and you are not quite sure of what you saw or how to explain it. Would you run in to town and tell everyone what you saw, and if you did, would they believe you?

One town in Alabama, after years and hundreds of reports of cryptid sightings, is embracing its Bigfoot heritage and hoping for a tourism boost by declaring itself the Bigfoot Capital of Alabama. Evergreen, in the southwest county of Conecuh, achieved this title when the city council passed this resolution in February 2017:

WHEREAS, many people around the world believe in the existence of Bigfoot-like creatures, and hundreds of sightings of these mysterious creatures are reported each year; and

WHEREAS, numerous Conecuh County residents have reported multiple sightings of mysterious Bigfoot-like creatures in and around Evergreen for decades, and that Evergreen is the geographical epicenter of these reported sightings; and

WHEREAS, those reports have attracted local, state, national and worldwide media attention, causing Evergreen and Conecuh County to be heavily associated with the ongoing discussion and study of Bigfoot reports in Alabama; and

WHEREAS, Evergreen and Conecuh County has attracted Bigfoot investigators from across the country, including members of the cast of the television show "Killing Bigfoot," to investigate reported Bigfoot sightings in the area, and leading them to find evidence of these creatures in the Evergreen area; and

WHEREAS, Bigfoot themed events have been heavily incorporated into large, public events like the annual Evergreen Collard Green Festival; and those Bigfoot themed events have attracted large crowds of interested, local Bigfoot enthusiasts to discuss Bigfoot sightings and evidence; and

WHEREAS, city officials recognize that many tourists, outdoor enthusiasts and visitors to Conecuh County are interested in Bigfoot and that those same visitors stop in Conecuh County in hopes of seeing one of these legendary creatures, and at the same time patronize area businesses, including local restaurants, hotels and gas stations while doing so; and

WHEREAS, local officials see the benefit of supporting the educational, social and tourism aspects of Bigfoot research; therefore be it

RESOLVED that I, Pete Wolff, Mayor of the City of Evergreen, do hereby declare the City of Evergreen, Alabama to be the Official Bigfoot Capital of Alabama; and be it further

RESOLVED, that the residents of Evergreen, Alabama and Conecuh County be encouraged to extend a friendly welcome to anyone visiting the area for purposes of learning more about local Bigfoot activity.

City of Evergreen officials with the senate proclamation naming Evergreen the "Bigfoot Capital of Alabama." *Courtesy of Lee Peacock.*

Since the town established itself as the Bigfoot Capital of Alabama, residents of Evergreen seem to be having fun with the concept. Local stores stock Bigfoot merchandise, and the council plans to put the moniker on Evergreen's welcome signs. The town hopes that embracing Bigfoot will be a draw for the area, Mayor Luther Upton told local television station WSFA: "It's the real deal. There's something out there. I think this will put Evergreen on the map as either the kookiest place in Alabama or the most interesting."

Evergreen is not the only place getting in on the Sasquatch action. Cheaha State Park, which has also had its fair share of reported sightings, has for a few years now sold merchandise such as stuffed Bigfoot toys, and magnets proclaiming, "I saw Bigfoot at Cheaha State Park." Park officials also put cartoon illustrations of the creature on park signs and named a popular hiking spot "Bigfoot Trail." In addition, a massive wooden Bigfoot statue greets park visitors.

Just remember, if you do happen to come across a Bigfoot in the wild, it is not a tourist attraction and needs to be left alone, just as our ancestors have throughout the history of the beasts' rumored existence.

16

ALABAMA WHITE THANG

Here's how one story goes:

When I was little my neighbor who was this little old lady told me and my cousin about the creature that roams around when it's midnight. She said twenty years ago two men who were hunting heard the screaming of either a woman or the loud crying of a baby, which is how this creature is supposed to sound. After being scared by the sounds, the men saw the White Thang, and when it noticed them, it took off after them running. The two hunters were scared and dropped their guns when they began to flee. They were unable to lose the beast and, in desperation, climbed a tree to escape. When the creature had them treed, it continued to circle the tree until the men threw down the raccoon they had shot earlier in the night. Satisfied with this meal, the monster turned and ran off into the woods. The hunters were so scared they stayed in the tree until the morning light covered the forest. They are not the only ones to encounter the White Thang either—my friend and his dad who live up on the mountain have said they have heard the beasts cry many times.

This describes an encounter with the legendary Alabama White Thang. For the past one hundred years, rumors and innuendo have swirled about run-ins with the creature. These tales seem to circulate heavily in north-central and northwestern parts of the state. The creature is described in a couple of different ways, the first being that of a fluffy, white creature that can stand upright but usually walks on all fours. It has a long, skinny tail ending in a furry ball.

This description goes with a story from an older Winston County resident on the website freestateofwinston.com. Feneda Martin said: "Old man George Norris…seen it over there in Enon graveyard, and he said it looked like a lion…you know, bushy, betwixt a dog and a lion. It was white and slick with long hair. It had a slick tail, down on the end of the tail a big ol' bush of hair."

This was not the only tale Feneda shared on the website. Another said:

Nathan Thomas said he had been to Florida, and he was coming back home and had been down there to see his brother. He caught a bus from Jasper to Nauvoo. He was walking out from Nauvoo, and they lived down in Kaeiser Bottoms. He was coming across the creek and up the hill just before you start down to Kaeiser Bottoms to their house, and he heard something "poomp" "poomp" "poomp" behind him. He looked back and [the White Thang] was coming after him just a-laying down. He said he broke and run and made it to get to a hickory tree and climbed it. He sat there until betwixt 1 to 2 o'clock in the morning. That thang layed down by

A display at Expedition Bigfoot in Blue Ridge, Georgia, shows a white Sasquatch head in comparison to other reported descriptions. *Author's collection.*

the tree and gnawed it. The moon was shining real bright, and sometime in the morning, it 'vantually gave up and walked away. He could see it way down the road. He said buddy I got down and I mean I run until I got to the house.

A second description for the White Thang's appearance says it is six to eight feet tall and bipedal, a small albino Bigfoot. The Alabama Bigfoot Society described a sighting similar to this by an unnamed woman in Blount County near Oneonta:

Her son says the creature was in a ditch and that he and the thing caught each other's attention at about the same time! They made eye contact for a few moments. He says they looked at each other eye to eye! But that it made no sound nor did it make any threatening move toward him. It simply walked slowly off into the dense forest. As it walked away he could then tell it was covered entirely with long solid white hair. The long hair fell over its face, and he could make out no other features than its eyes.

Though the physical descriptions may vary, the creature has some features in common:

- They are bright white to light gray in color.
- They can move exceedingly fast for their size.
- They have a shrill shriek that can be mistaken for a woman screaming, a baby crying or possibly the sound of a mountain lion.

Some researchers say the Alabama White Thang is probably an albino bear or an albino mountain lion, while some will go so far as to say that it is an albino sasquatch. There is even the occasional theory that the White Thang is the spirit of a long-dead sasquatch or bear.

There is little history about the origins of the White Thang, other than the fact that it likely stems from Bigfoot legends or other variants in differing parts of the country.

The Alabama White Thang Facebook page features recent reports of encounters:

My girlfriend just saw this thing in Florence near Wildwood Park by an abandoned house that has collapsed in and it fits the description perfectly.

She saw it standing upright and ran away on all fours but hopped like a deer. —Mackie G. October 2017.

My true story. I was about 14 yrs old. We came home for vacation one summer. That first morning I had to go to the bathroom. On my way back to bed I heard something outside, looking out the window it was sooo foggy thick. But a few feet from the house I saw the WHITEST critter just standing there red eyes, it was standing like a kangaroo would I saw the blackest claws the more I stared at it I could see the shape of it. I was frozen. Until my grandmother Norton said what is it. I told her what Was out there. Seeing this critter ruined my vacation. I was afraid to go outside. When I did I was constantly looking over my shoulder. My grandmother told me another story about this thing that happened to my grandfather. All this happened in Courtland, AL. —Angie B. September 2017

Yes, I saw one in 1985. This was no albino bigfoot because I was close enough to see light brown hair mixed in with the white. It seemed to be transitioning from white to brown. Nothing about what I saw that night made sense to me. I first thought I had walked up on a neighbor's cow that had gotten loose. Nope. It was not anything I was familiar with. I've been around animals all my life and I knew what this thing wasn't. —Regina A. October 2017

Regardless of whether you believe in the White Thang, it makes a fabulous rural legend that is uniquely Alabama.

17

HUGGIN' MOLLY

SHE'LL HUG YOU TO DEATH

I know the story by heart. I've been hearing it since I was kid: "Don't stay out after dark, or Huggin' Molly will get you and hug you to death." People would say,

> *I know it's true because my grandmother told me about her friend that it happened to when she was ten years old. She had stayed out after dark, and she wasn't far from home, so she wasn't scared about being out so late. She was walking down the road that would take her to her backyard, and she was in sight of her house when Huggn' Molly stepped in front of her from out of nowhere. The girl screamed and ran around the large woman dressed in black and ran home. She ran in the back door and locked it as her mom came in and asked what happened when the girl said that she had seen Huggin' Molly. The only thing the girl's mother had to say was "I told you not to stay out after dark or Huggin' Molly would get you."*

In Abbeville, the legend of Huggin' Molly has a long history with local children. It was passed down from one generation of parents to the next as a warning to keep children inside after dark.

As with all legends, this one has variations. The most common telling of the legend is that Huggin' Molly was a real woman thought to be a witch. She was seven feet tall and dressed all in black, wandering the streets at night looking for children who stayed out after dark. When she found them,

Has this unknown woman on a porch in Abbeville seen Huggin' Molly? *Library of Congress.*

she would hug the life from them while screaming in their ears. Then she would take them to her lair for some nefarious purpose.

Another version of the legend is the one told by Huggin' Molly's restaurant in Abbeville, which is named for the legend. The eatery's website says,

> *The versions of who Huggin' Molly actually was vary. But one frequent description depicts her as a giant of a woman, maybe 7 feet tall and as big around as a bale of cotton. Some say her ghost still walks the streets of Abbeville late in the night, sweeping her black skirt as she goes. If she happens upon you, she chases you down, gives you a huge hug and screams in your ear.*

The owner of Huggin' Molly's, Jimmy Rane, chose the name, the restaurant's website says. "Jimmy Rane, an Abbeville native and lifelong resident, grew up hearing the legend of Huggin' Molly. For him and his friends, she was as real as the trees that rustled in the wind at night."

"Anybody who grew up in Abbeville grew up knowing the legend of Huggin' Molly," Jimmy said. "If your mother or dad didn't want you to be out after dark, they'd tell you Huggin' Molly would get you. And you believed it, too."

The website continues:

> *One night, Jimmy and his good friend Tommy Murphy heard the story from Tommy's dad. He told them he knew Huggin' Molly was real because she had sprung from the shadows and hugged him one night. They were convinced it had to be true. To this day, hearts beat faster as the moon rises in the sky over Abbeville. Huggin' Molly, dressed all in black, could show up at any time.*

Another version of the Huggin' Molly legend says that she is the spirit of a professor at the former Southeast Alabama Agriculture School who in the afterlife is trying to keep students safe by keeping them off the streets at night. Another version of this story is that she is the ghost of a woman whose infant child died, and she is trying to keep children from danger on the streets.

One other legend is told in the book *Legends, Lore & True Tales of the Chattahoochee* by Michelle Smith. According to Smith, Huggin' Molly was a real person; as a small child, she had her arm removed and was given a golden arm as a replacement. As Molly grew up, several boys in town were said to be waiting for her death so that they could take her golden arm. After Molly's death and funeral, the boys dug up her body and removed the arm. As the boys began to fill in the grave, a voice rose from the tomb, saying, "I want my golden arm!" The boys ran from the grave, but the voice followed them, yelling, "Come back, come back!" During the chase, one of the boys was grabbed from behind by the black-robed woman, who squeezed him until he couldn't breathe then screamed loudly in his ear until he thought he might die of shock. The other boys fought with the woman to free their friend, and when he was released, the group fled home to escape the woman, taking the arm with them.

The boys later melted down Molly's golden arm and sold it in pieces, but Molly still roams the street grabbing children in search of the boys who stole her golden arm. This story is derived from an age-old campfire tale called "The Golden Arm."

Some histories of the Huggin' Molly legend claim a separate hooded lady in black roams the streets of Abbeville and nearby Headland, tormenting both children and adults. This particular legend does not include Molly's hugging or screaming or describe her as being large, but residents in both towns seem to be in agreement that Huggin' Molly and the Hooded Lady in Black are versions of the same legend.

Some believed that Huggin' Molly was a witch. Witch fervor spread through the New World during parts of the seventeenth and eighteenth centuries. *Library of Congress.*

The legend of Huggin' Molly is so well known that in addition to the restaurant, it has also inspired a 2017 song by Odilon Green. In the liner notes, the artist said:

So I've decided that any time I don't have a different specific song in mind but want to keep progressing towards the dream of hitting 50, I'm going to do another song in my "Local Legends" series about cryptids. Starting with Alabama (this song) and progressing alphabetically through all 50 states (or as many as I get to), I am going to do a song about the monsters, ghosts and strange sightings of modern American lore. To launch the series, here's a fun little kids' ditty called "The Scream of Huggin' Molly" based on, obviously, the Alabama legend about the title character.

Molly screams for you
Huggin' Molly's wandering the dark tonight
Molly screams for you
Huggin' Molly's reaching out for you tonight

Jimmy snuck out of his home real late
It was a hot summer night and it seemed like a great
Opportunity to just hang out under the stars
Mom and Dad wouldn't approve but he wouldn't go far

But though the streets had been deserted he saw someone ahead
A figure seven-foot-tall that filled him with dread
Dressed all in black, and a face well hidden
By the darkness underneath a hat's wide brim

Jimmy turned the other way but the figure was there
He was caught in a ghostly pale woman's stare
She wrapped her arms around him and held him in place
Not a hug like his Mom's but a cold embrace

He struggled to get free but her arms were like steel
The thought sprang into his head he might be her next meal
The woman opened her mouth, leaned her face in near
Then let loose a mighty shriek right into his ear

Alabama Lore

Molly screams for you
Huggin' Molly's looking for the kids tonight
Molly screams for you
Huggin' Molly wants to hold you tonight

They found Jimmy the next morning with tears in his eyes
Shook up by his night before but very much alive
When they asked him what had happened he didn't respond
All he could hear was echoes of her scream go on and on

But old man Henry down the road said don't be alarmed
It was just ol' Huggin' Molly and she means no harm
Though Jimmy's ears are ringing now it will fade in a day
It is Molly who is stuck in a wretched way

She lost her own infant many lifetimes past
So spends all time hoping to find her baby at last
When a child walks alone at night she will appear
And hoping it is hers, she will hug it near

So don't blame Molly if she lets out a wail
When her hopes once again are to no avail
When a person spends eternity in their own hell
I think we can forgive them if they need to yell.

© 2017 Odilon Green

18

THE STRANGE CASE OF THE CHOCCOLOCCO MONSTER

Have you heard the tale of a creature that roams the woods of Calhoun County east of Anniston near Iron City?

The strange figure is said to be the lost spirit of a young Native American brave who, on special nights each year, is given a living form to return to his woodlands.

The legend began in an unusually bad winter in the late 1700s, when wild game became scarce near an Indian village, leading braves to venture farther into the woods to hunt. One day, a young brave ventured much too far from home and became lost in the woods. He decided to spend the night and retrace his steps the next morning. Overnight, the snow covered all traces of his trail. The brave wandered the woods in vain trying to find his way back to the village but soon starved to death. When on the verge of death, the brave was visited by a wood spirit that would help him pass into the next world. This same spirit is said to have allowed the brave to return to earth on certain nights to hunt for his tribe. But the brave does not return in his human form. Instead, he returns as a large beast. The skin is gone from his head, and large horns have sprouted. Seeing the creature in the woods is said to be a bad omen and means impending doom for someone close to you.

This fabricated tale is just one explanation behind an Alabama mystery that took almost four decades to solve—the case of the Choccolocco Monster.

In the spring of 1969, as Americans were fascinated with a space program that would shortly put a man on the moon for the first time, residents in the mostly rural area of Calhoun County known as Choccolocco were transfixed with something else: a monster in their midst. It started in mid-May of that year on a county road running between Iron City and Choccolocco. Before this sighting, there had been no reports of a creature roaming these woods, other than the occasional reports of Bigfoot or pukwudgie, which didn't fit the description of the Choccolocco Monster.

Local resident Margaret Teague was driving home from work late one evening when she saw a creature just to the edge of the road. She referred to it as a "booger," which has long been a nickname for the sasquatch that are said to roam this area of the lower Appalachian Mountains. In an interview with the *Anniston Star* newspaper, she described the animal as large and bipedal with an oversized head. Her exact words were "Oh, Lordy, Lordy, what a head." Unsure of what she'd seen, she attempted to get another look at it. "I turned the car around in the middle of the road to get another look, and it got caught in the ditch, I just knowed [*sic*] the booger had me for sure." Thankfully, the creature ran off.

More than a week later, an unnamed man reported what he called a "varmint" resembling a humpbacked cross between a panther and a bear. The next night, in the same location, Johnny Ray Teague and three friends were checking the engine of their car on the side of the road when the monster again made its appearance known. First came the sounds of crashing through the brush and then the appearance of a huge head with large, prominent teeth, "the size of a cow, gray to black in color, humped similarly to a camel." The men jumped into the car and locked the door and watched as the beast circled the car a few times before lumbering off into the woods. Teague was finally able to get his car started, and the quartet fled the scene. Less than a mile down the road, the men encountered three or four more of the creatures, all larger than the first.

Over the next few weeks, various sightings of the creature were reported to authorities. Some witnesses described the creature as gray or black, with large teeth and a hump. Others added that it had long, stringy hair that obscured its features. No one appears to have gotten a good view of the weird creature.

After the initial reports, June 1969 saw an influx of curious hunters to the area who were patrolling the roads at night to shoot the creature and solve the mystery. There were so many people with guns that local farmers worried their livestock would be inadvertently mistaken for the creature and shot, which fortunately did not come to pass.

One June night, the creature lumbered in front of an approaching truck. The vehicle slowed so someone inside could fire several shots from a rifle.

The beast fled through the woods as the hunters flooded the area with spotlights. The hunter or hunters involved were never named, but one was quoted in the paper saying that the monster ran back into the hills, letting out "an almost humanlike cry." After that, sightings stopped, and the legend faded into folklore.

Thirty-two years later, the truth behind the Choccolocco Monster finally surfaced. *Anniston Star* reporter Matthew Creamer brought the decades-old tale to the forefront with the exclusive Halloween Day report that Nances Creek resident Neal Williamson was behind the creatures' mysterious appearances.

One boring weekend night, Williamson, who was then fifteen years old, took his parents' truck and was riding around the county back roads when he spotted a cow skull in the cab, giving him an idea to alleviate his boredom. He donned the cow skull and a long black coat, waiting alongside a long dark stretch of road and watching for cars. As the cars approached, he ran into the street and danced around before running back into the trees so the car's occupants would not get a good look at him. He did this several times to different cars. At times, instead of the black jacket, he wore a white sheet. His adaptation of the creature ended that June night when he and some buddies he let in on the secret jumped out in front of the wrong truck. Instead of being scared, the people in this truck started shooting at him as he ran through the woods and pastures to escape.

While this revelation should have brought an end to tales of the Choccolocco Monster, it would soon take on a life of its own. When researching news topics for *The Daily Show with John Stewart*, producers came across the tale of the fake creature and brought a camera crew to the small unincorporated town of Nances Creek. They filmed a short piece on the trickery, which aired nationally in December 2001 on the Comedy Central show. This made a fun and fitting end to a long-running urban legend of a mythical creature.

19

GHOSTLY GOVERNOR THOMAS BIBB AND HIS HAUNTED FAMILY

Tales of ghostly rulers go back to the beginning of organized society. It seems that some rulers want to continue their reign long after their deaths. Here in the United States, the ghosts of former presidents Andrew Jackson and Abraham Lincoln are rumored to haunt the White House. It should be no surprise, then, to learn then that Alabama has a tale of a dearly departed governor whose restless spirit roams the night. He doesn't haunt a manor or governor's residence but a cemetery that once aspired to be the burial grounds for Alabama governors.

If you happen to find yourself in Huntsville's Maple Hill Cemetery on the night of a full moon, search for the grave of Thomas Bibb. Watch closely, and you will behold an amazing sight—a black carriage driven by white horses pulling up to its edge, Thomas crawling from his resting place and climbing into the buggy, leading it around Maple Hill Cemetery and trying to find a way to get home to his beloved Belle Mina country estate.

Bibb was the president of the Constitutional Congress that created Alabama's Constitution in 1819, the final step to statehood. He then took over as president of the state senate. He was serving in this position in 1820 when his older brother, William Wyatt Bibb, who had been elected the year before to be the state's first governor, died in office. The newly written constitution declared that a governor who was no longer able to serve was to be replaced by the president of the state senate, which made Thomas Bibb Alabama's second governor.

Legend has it that Thomas Bibb climbs out of this grave on the night of a full moon. *Author's collection.*

He had an unremarkable run as governor but did oversee two important parts of Alabama history: First, he named Cahaba the state's first official capital city and changed the name of Cahaba County to Bibb County in honor of his brother. Thomas also oversaw the legislature responsible for approving the development of the first state-run bank. Thomas did not run for reelection in 1821, deciding instead to return to cotton farming.

Records show he continued his cotton business, served in the Alabama House of Representatives in 1828 and 1829 and was the director of the Huntsville Branch of the Bank of the State of Alabama. He also oversaw completion of his plantation, Belle Mina, in Limestone County. But accounts vary on details surrounding his death in 1839. Some reports say that he died in Belle Mina, some indicate he died in Mobile and still others say he passed away in New Orleans, Louisiana.

One legend attached to Thomas's death in New Orleans has made the rounds over the years. His family, knowing he wanted to be buried on the property of his beloved Belle Mina, tried to figure out how to get his body from southern Louisiana to northern Alabama in the best shape possible. They decided to preserve his body in a barrel of whiskey for the train journey. Upon his arrival, he was laid out in Athens for viewers

BELLE MINA

Thomas Bibb built this grand house in 1826 and named it "Belle Manor" (beautiful home), but local pronunciation altered it to "Belle Mina". The home which stayed in the Bibb family until 1940 was the seat of Bibb's large plantation, and furnished the name of the small town nearby. The town of Belle Mina developed around a railroad station intended for the nearby town of Mooresville, the residents of which didn't want it built too close to their homes and businesses.

While serving as President of the Alabama Senate, Thomas Bibb ascended to the office of Governor when his brother William Wyatt Bibb, then holding that office was accidentally killed in a fall from his horse. William Wyatt Bibb had been Governor of Alabama Territory 1817-1819, and when statehood was granted he became the first Governor of the State of Alabama.

ERECTED BY
LIMESTONE COUNTY HISTORICAL SOCIETY &
ATHENS/LIMESTONE TOURISM COUNCIL 2003

This historic marker is at the site of Thomas Bibb's Belle Mina former plantation home. Limestone County Historical Association.

to pay their last respects before he was buried in the family cemetery at Belle Mina.

So how did he come to be interred in Maple Hill Cemetery? Huntsville's town fathers, who wanted Maple Hill to be the resting place of Alabama's governors, requested Bibb be exhumed from Belle Mina and reinterred in Maple Hill. But the legend says because Thomas's wish was to be buried at Belle Mina, his restless soul rides the cemetery under the light of the full moon, searching for a way back.

Another legend surrounds the naming of Thomas's Belle Mina. In multiple documents, the home was referred to as Belmina, with no explanation for the name, and the spelling gradually changed to "Belle Mina." Another story says Thomas originally named his plantation Belle Manor, using the French word *belle*, meaning beautiful. The name was inadvertently changed when census takers in the latter part of the 1800s could not understand southern drawls and heard "Belle Manor" as "Belle Mina" and spelled it that way on historical records.

Bibb also had a city home in downtown Huntsville, Alabama, where some family members also lived. And it is here that legends about Bibb's daughter-in-law grew.

In fact, while Thomas Bibb was more famous in life, his daughter-in-law Mary Bibb has a more popular reputation in the world of urban legends.

Mary's story is one of young love turned to tragedy. In 1835, nineteen-year-old Mary Chambers, the daughter of a local doctor, married William D. Bibb, son of the former governor. She was a lively and well-liked young woman, one who enjoyed sitting on the front porch of her home in her favorite rocking chair, greeting and chatting with friends and neighbors. While getting ready for her wedding day, Mary was inadvertently poisoned and became violently ill after the wedding. She clung to life for about six weeks before succumbing to her illness.

Both the Chambers and Bibb sides of the family were distressed at this unfortunate turn of events. The Bibb family ordered the construction of the first mausoleum in Maple Hill Cemetery as Mary's final resting place.

The family wanted a mausoleum instead of a grave so that Mary could be buried in her wedding dress, with her beloved rocking chair at her graveside. It is this rocking chair that drives the legend of Mary Bibb. Legend says those who visit the mausoleum and knock three times on its side will hear the sounds of Mary's chair creaking as it rocks.

While many stories were written about the wedding of the governor's son and his beautiful young bride, few details survive about the origins of the poison that killed Mary. Some legends say that she was using arsenic-based powder to make herself very pale, as was the fashion of the day. Yet

The mausoleum of Mary Chambers Bibb at Maple Hill Cemetery in Huntsville. *Author's collection.*

The author's son is testing the legend of Mary Bibb's rocking chair. *Author's collection.*

Thomas Bibb's former town home in Huntsville, pictured here around 1945, is supposedly haunted by his granddaughter Adeline Bibb. *Library of Congress.*

another story says one of the servants attending Mary during her wedding preparation inadvertently gave her poison instead of her medication. This version of the story seems the most plausible, even though the type of medicine and type of poison change with each recorded version of the story.

Historians seem to agree that Mary was likely buried in her wedding dress, given the short time between her nuptials and her death. As for the rocking chair, no records exist to show it was there, and the mausoleum is completely sealed, so going inside is not a possibility.

Many historians in the area think that the rocking chair is not really in the mausoleum. They hoped to put the question to rest when maintenance to its roof was required in the early 2000s, but when the roof was lifted, workers saw the structure was also sealed from the top. The truth may never be known.

While the lives of Thomas and Mary Bibb provide plenty of fodder for urban legends and ghost stories, there is one other Bibb rumored to haunt Huntsville.

Adeline Bibb's spirit is said to wander the grounds of another Bibb home in downtown Huntsville. Adeline's spirit is said to be restless because she received the house as a gift from her father, and her husband, James Bradley, lost it in a poker game. According to lore, Adeline learned her home was no longer hers when she returned from errands and found a man pulling flowers from the garden. When she confronted him, she was told the new owners did not like the flowers and asked for their removal.

The reality of the situation is just as harsh as the truth, but not as entertaining. Adeline's husband, James Bradley, purchased the home from Thomas Bibb in 1836 for the very generous family member price of $5,000. Bradley co-owned the commission merchants Martin Pleasants & Company, which held large tracts of land throughout the south. The 1837 economic downturn set the company on the road to ruin until Thomas stepped in and provided money to help keep the business afloat. He continued this until his death in 1839, racking up over $600,000 in debt that fell to his heirs upon his death. Unable to keep the creditors at bay, James and Adeline were forced to sell the house in 1844 to avoid financial catastrophe.

20

HARTSELLE'S CRY BABY HOLLOW

This is a story that I heard repeatedly while growing up in north Alabama, although it seemed to change a little depending on who was doing the telling. Several other counties, including Marshall County, where I was raised, have similar versions of the tale. Now that I think about it, every state that I have resided in has a similar story about Cry Baby Hollow.

You've probably heard the tale: it's about a one-lane bridge in the woods in a rural area of the county. Everyone says if you go there at night and stop on the bridge, you can hear a baby crying. Legend has it that the baby was drowned in the creek by its mother, who was insane and thought the baby was evil.

Perhaps you have heard the disturbing legend that Native Americans who inhabited this area long ago would take their sick infants down to a particular creek and drown them or leave them to die. This resulted in a well-worn trail through the area, and as the area was settled, the trail became a road with a bridge. Now, the story goes, you can hear the crying of lost infants if you stop on the bridge at night.

Another version of the story says that if you stop your car on the bridge, the ghostly headlights of a black sedan will appear from nowhere and chase your car from the area. The apparition is reportedly driven by the ghost of a person killed in a car in the first part of the twentieth century, and the spirit doesn't want others to meet the same fate.

Yet another version says that if you leave a candy bar on the edge of the bridge and leave, you will find a bite has been taken out of it when you return. You may also hear an infant crying or a woman sobbing. This legend reportedly stemmed from an incident in the 1800s when a wagon crossing a wooden bridge in the same location crashed, sending a young mother and her infant child into the creek below. The infant drowned in the waters while the mother survived. Mysterious sounds are attributed to the cries of the baby and the weeping of the grief-stricken mother. Still another tale says if you go to the bridge and stop your car briefly before driving away, you will later find tiny handprints from a ghostly child covering your vehicle. The child in this tale allegedly died in the 1950s or 1960s in a car accident on the bridge.

This tale is my favorite: If you go to the bridge, turn off your headlights and put your car in neutral, it will be pushed across the bridge by a young woman who was killed by a motor vehicle while walking along the bridge. She reportedly pushes your car across the bridge to keep you from the same fate.

These legends surround the same place, a small bridge on a county road in Hartselle, Alabama. The area is known as Cry Baby Hollow. In other counties, such legendary spots may be called cry baby holler, cry baby bridge or cry baby creek.

Numerous people have shared experiences of the bridge online. The website HauntedPlaces.org has many commenters about the site:

Every time I go at night there seems to be a vehicle that pops up out of nowhere and does the same. I even had a mysterious encounter with a ghost train. I swear this on my life and it scared the hell out of me. —Devin

I grew up around this area, and I know the legend goes that Indians would put babies there I can't remember why…and that you can still hear them crying. Mom told me that when I was little that if you would put a candy bar on the bridge the "babies" would get it and eat it. —Kelly

I went there with my brothers and a boyfriend when I was younger about 15 yrs ago. We was told the stories and that we should put a candy bar on the bridge and wait and it would be gone before you know it. Well sure enough when we did that it was gone and then we saw a ghostly figure in the water and got in the truck to leave and there was baby hand prints on the wind shield. I strongly believe in ghost 100% I have seen my own family after they pass away. This was one of the scariest thing I have ever witnessed in my life! So its true!! —Anonymous

The famed bridge in Cry Baby Hollow in Hartselle is a little less than impressive but is a magnet for graffiti. *Author's collection.*

Ok. I'm not really a believer in ghost and stuff but this bridge has baffled me. Me and some friends went 3 separate times this week and each time we would bring a new friend and put a half-eaten Baby Ruth on the bridge and come back in a few minutes and make them pick it up! It scares the hell out of em! BUT, each time I have been and iv been 5 times in 3 nights and each time there would be hand prints all over the door and bed of my truck. There was never a thumb print it was ALWAYS 4 fingers rubbing down or sideways down my truck. This fact is indisputable and I can't explain it. —David

Even with these experiences and stories spanning more than seventy-five years, there is no recorded proof of any such tragedy involving a baby occurring in this area. There have been vehicular accidents—many of which involve people testing the legends—but none similar to the ones that inspired the tales.

This seems to be the case with similar stories throughout Alabama, as well as across the United States. A quick internet search turns up well over one hundred bridges with this legend attached.

This is the creek in Cry Baby Hollow from which the sounds of a crying baby are said to rise. *Author's collection.*

The bridges seem to have several things in common:

- They are one-lane bridges over creeks or bodies of water that do appear creepy.
- They are in rural areas.
- They attract people who try to add to the legends and scare others with graffiti.

No one knows of any particular person related to the haunting, with all legends referring to an unnamed baby and, at times, an unknown mother.

Theories about the origins of these legends are as varied as the tales themselves. Some say they are cautionary tales warning people from dangerous bridges in rural areas. Whatever their origins, stories such as these predate the invention of the automobile.

But rest assured, most any young person in a county with such a legend can direct you to the bridge at its center. It is even a pretty good bet that whoever you ask will be glad to share their own experience of the haunted hollow and the forever crying baby.

21

THE SPIRITS OF
OLD GEORGIA CEMETERY

One of my favorite things to do when visiting Huntsville Hospital is start a conversation with people in the elevator. I always ask, "Did you know Huntsville Hospital is built on top of a cemetery?" I am met with surprise 99 percent of the time. I follow up by asking if they have watched the movie *Poltergeist*. Those who have seen the movie know why this is funny—it is about a family that moves into a house built on top of a cemetery and is haunted by the spirits of those interred there.

Unlike in *Poltergeist*, Huntsville Hospital does not seem to have malevolent spirits walking its halls, although there are whispers of unexplained events and rumors of paranormal activity. I spoke with a former hospital security officer (who asked to remain anonymous) who recalled an event that occurred when she was checking empty patient rooms. She walked into an empty room and turned on the light, and there was a man lying on the bed. He turned his head and looked at her. She apologized for disturbing him and looked at the door number to make sure she was in the correct room. When she turned her attention back into the room, the man was gone. Fearing this was a patient who had wondered into the wrong room, she searched but no one was in there. This is the most detailed description I've come across of spirits in the hospital, which makes sense—stories of a haunted hospital would not be good for business.

Rest assured that Huntsville Hospital doesn't *really* sit on top of a cemetery; the graves were moved prior to construction. The cemetery in question was founded in 1818 as a city cemetery, although at the time, it was outside the city limits. It became known locally as the Georgia Cemetery, Georgia Graveyard or Old Georgia Graveyard. The Georgia part of the name reportedly came from the slaves who were brought to Huntsville from Georgia.

A historical marker erected in 2001 on the northeast corner of the hospital gives a brief description:

> On September 3, 1818, the Huntsville City Commissioners purchased two acres of land from LeRoy Pope for a "burying ground" for slaves. This cemetery was located within the NE quarter of Section 1, Township 4, Range 1 West of the Base Meridian. It was affectionately known as "Georgia" within the black community. The cemetery continued to be used from 1818 until 1870 when Glenwood Cemetery was designated as the city's burial ground for African Americans. No known records have survived.

While this marker states that the land was purchased for the purpose of being a burying ground for slaves, the marker is incorrect. The land was purchased for a city cemetery, not specifically for a slave cemetery. It is believed that both white and black people were buried in the cemetery, but the area was prone to flooding and the city quickly abandoned white burials at the site, moving them to Maple Hill Cemetery. The less-desirable Georgia Cemetery became the burying ground for black residents. The cemetery became a gathering spot for local slaves, especially for worship services.

Beginning in about 1820, Elder William Harris was said to have given powerful sermons of hope and encouragement to lift the spirits of the slaves. These services continued and grew along with the cemetery, and soon Harris was able to construct a chapel among the graves for the worship services.

The new church was known as the Huntsville African Baptist Church and was the start of what is now recognized as the oldest black church in the state of Alabama. It is also the first Primitive Baptist Church known to be organized *by* black man *for* black people.

The church was active for the next several decades as the cemetery grew, and families planted trees in honor of their loved ones. A church history referred to the location as "the silent city of the dead, with its church for the living" and the congregation loved the church, attending services there until the Union invasion of Huntsville in 1862 during the War Between the States.

During the occupation of Huntsville, the small church in the cemetery was burned. After the war, funds for rebuilding the church were allocated by the U.S. government, and construction began in about 1871 at a new location on Fountain Row in downtown Huntsville.

The church on Fountain Row was dedicated in 1872 and came with a new name—Saint Bartley Primitive Baptist Church, after its pastor, Elder Bartley Harris, who was known for his saintly behavior. Harris is famous in Huntsville history for having baptized more than three thousand people in the town's Big Spring, at the site where the city was founded. The church was located on this site for the next ninety-two years before being relocated and rebuilt. A historical marker at the former site of this church says:

> *Organized 1820 by William Harris, a slave, who was minister more than 50 years. Original church, called Huntsville African Baptist, stood 4 blocks south in Old Georgia Graveyard. In 1870, this church and 3 others formed Indian Creek Primitive Baptist Association. Congregation occupied brick church on this site 1872–1964. In 1965, moved to new building, 3020 Belafonte Ave., N.W. Present name honors Bartley Harris, saintly second minister. Other pastors: Felix Jordan, Eli Patton, Richard Moore, Amos Robinson.*

That's the story of the church and its pastor, but few records have been located to tell what became of the cemetery. One rumor says that the land on which the cemetery was located was deeded to the Huntsville African Baptist Church by the city, while another says the church purchased the land.

Another legend says that Bartley Harris sold the cemetery and surrounding grounds back to the city for expansion, with a clause saying the cemetery would stay and be maintained by the city. Shortly after the deal was signed, the contract was lost, and when it turned up a few weeks later, any mention of keeping the cemetery was gone. The bodies were disinterred in 1870, with most being relocated to the newly formed African American Glenwood Cemetery.

Another version of the story says that the city never relinquished ownership of the land, and in 1870, when Glenwood Cemetery was established, the bodies from Georgia Cemetery were exhumed against protests of the black community and moved to the new location. This paved the way for future development of the land.

Which stories are true? The answer will likely forever remain a mystery, as there no longer seem to be records from that time.

According to area historians, there were no official records kept for the Old Georgia Cemetery, so no one knows exactly who or how many people were buried there. The Historic Huntsville Foundation says this about the body removals: "As no one kept burial records of those buried in Georgia, it is unknown how many graves were moved from the Georgia cemetery to Glenwood and how many bodies remain in the ground beneath the hospital complex."

In addition, Saint Bartley Harris Primitive Baptist Church historians say that while the city claims burials in Georgia Cemetery ceased in 1870, before the bodies were removed and relocated to Glenwood Cemetery, congregants said that burials continued at the site through the turn of the twentieth century.

Whatever the case, we do know that historic Glenwood Cemetery is the final resting place of at least some of those people moved from the Old Georgia Graveyard. A historical marker at the new cemetery says,

> *Glenwood Cemetery was established in 1870 by the City of Huntsville following the purchase of 10 acres from the Benjamin W. Blake estate, originally a part of the John Brahan Plantation. Additional land was added in 1875 from the W.W. Darwin family, resulting in the current configuration. Distinguished African Americans buried here include veterans of America's wars beginning with the Civil War, former slaves, accomplished artisans, professionals in many fields, clergymen, educators, entrepreneurs, politicians, and other leaders.*

City officials say Old Georgia Cemetery was located under what is today the parking garage for Huntsville Hospital, but old-timers from Saint Bartleys Primitive Baptist Church say that the cemetery extended much farther south, under what is now the main portion of the facility, and the descriptions of the cemetery and its size seem to support the church's theory.

A final creepy thought: The hospital's morgue is located in the underground basement of the main building, which was most likely built over the top of the old grave sites—something to think about on your next visit.

22

THE MYSTERIOUS TOWN OF COTTONPORT AND ITS LONG-DEAD INHABITANTS

There is a small cemetery on the back roads of New Hope, Alabama, with some unusual and mysterious graves. A sign directs drivers to the burials and a large wooden sign that reads "Unknown Graves brought from Limestone Co. in 1968." The sign stands watch over 194 granite markers bearing only a single number each. There is a mention of these graves in the historical marker at the cemetery: "During the construction of Interstate 65 in 1968, remains from the Collier Cemetery in Limestone County were reinterred at Hayden." This is not a lot of information about these mysterious graves, so what's the story behind them, and whose bodies are buried beneath the numbered markers?

If you are ever driving south on Interstate 65, just before you cross the Tennessee River, you'll notice how wild the land along its banks seems today. To the left, away from the Decatur side, you will be looking at a piece of hidden north Alabama history—an area that was once known as the town of Cottonport. All that remains of the town today are the words on one side of a historic marker:

> *The town of Cottonport flourished in the early years of Limestone County. It was settled in 1818 and chartered in 1824. It was located approx. 1½ miles S.E. near the point where Limestone Creek flowed into the Tennessee River and was a prime boat landing. Steamboats from E. Tennessee brought much needed goods to this area. During high water, flatboats loaded with bales of cotton departing Cottonport, could cross the river's rocky shoals and float to New Orleans.*

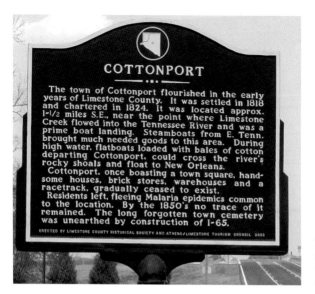

This historical marker is all that remains near what was once the town of Cottonport. *Author's collection.*

Cottonport's location along the river was advantageous to farmers, who would come from neighboring communities to load their crops and cotton on barges. River traffic helped the small port town flourish. Multiple warehouses for cotton and other goods were built, a town square was formed and many homes dotted the landscape. The town even boasted a racetrack, where locals and river traders would gather for entertainment and the occasional wager.

The town's riverside location would soon become its curse. While men were traveling the waterways, mosquitoes were busy breeding along its banks. This led to outbreaks of malaria, driving settlers farther inland to escape the disease-carrying insects. Cottonport's residents may also have suffered from yellow fever outbreaks, which twice devastated the neighboring community of Decatur.

So many people died or fled that the town was soon abandoned. By the 1850s, no trace of the town remained, and it was largely forgotten—until graves were unearthed by construction of I-65 more than one hundred years later.

Cottonport and its quick decline have been researched by many historians, but little information has been found about its residents. Due to its location near Huntsville, the state's first temporary capital, some of the state's earliest and wealthiest settlers could have resided in the town or at least had business dealings there. No one knows what happened to the many buildings that formed the town or the destinations of the residents who fled the town.

Did yellow fever help end the city of Cottonport? *Library of Congress.*

In 1968, as I-65 was being constructed through Limestone County, a grader uncovered 12 bodies near the Tennessee River. The coffins had long since deteriorated, and there were no markers, leaving confused state officials to call a halt to construction and try to find information on the graves. What they found was 183 more bodies—but no records. Historians decided the state had uncovered the cemetery of the lost town of Cottonport. This could also have been named the Tucker Graveyard at Cottonport, which was mentioned in historian Faye Axford's book *The Lure and Lore of Limestone County*. This seems to be the only known recorded mention of a cemetery in the now-obscure town.

Unable to reroute I-65 around the cemetery, the state advertised the discovery and asked that any relatives or anyone with information come forward. When no one did, state officials requested bids from cemeteries statewide with room to reinter the bodies. The owners of Hayden Cemetery in New Hope won the bid.

The 195 bodies were excavated from the construction site, placed in wooden boxes, documented, transported the fifty miles to New Hope and reinterred at Hayden Cemetery, where they have become a curiosity.

Strangely, the numbers on the graves are not in order but randomly placed on the rows of graves. The historical marker at Hayden Cemetery mistakenly says the bodies came from Collier Cemetery in Limestone County, which may have been the belief in 1968.

Now for a final mystery: If you have been reading closely, you have noticed that 195 bodies were exhumed, but only 194 were reinterred. What happened to the remaining body? Was it taken for forensic study or historical recording purposes in a museum? The answer only leads to more questions.

The bodies had been reduced to skeletons, as the wooden boxes and burial clothes had deteriorated over time—all except one. The workers doing the excavations came upon a cast-iron casket, supposedly a Springfield model 92. Cast-iron caskets were popular before and during the Civil War, but only the wealthiest of families were able to purchase them. They can be seen today in museums, and occasionally, one will pop up for sale on eBay.

The cast-iron coffin discovered in Limestone County was intact and featured a glass viewing window where the corpse's head would be. Once the glass was cleaned, workers could make out the remains of a corpse and a suit of clothes with a diamond pin in the lapel.

The casket and its contents were reported as being loaded with the other remains and taken to Hayden cemetery in New Hope. But it was never reinterred.

Are there any remains of the town of Cottonport under this swampy area? *Library of Congress.*

This is the final resting place of most of Cottonport's residents, fifty miles away in New Hope. *Author's collection.*

It seems the remains of the 194 bodies and the iron casket were left in the transport truck overnight at Hayden Cemetery for burial the next day, but the following morning, the iron casket was gone.

There are varying tales of what became of the casket and the man inside. One legend says it was stolen for the diamond stickpin. Another, more plausible story says that the morning of the burial, cemetery owners received word from a state agency that officials wanted to study the casket and the remains. A New Hope historian thinks the state department of forensics made the request, but no state agency has ever confirmed receiving the casket or remains.

Since the cast-iron casket was lost, rumors have swirled concerning its whereabouts, with some people postulating that an X-files agency or FBI group nabbed it for examination.

While Cottonport is famous for its enduring mysteries, it is not the only noted Limestone County town to simply vanish. Bridgewater was another town lost to history. It was recorded as being located along the Elk River in Alabama, fifteen miles south of Elkton, Tennessee, and ten miles above Fort Hampton at Simms Landing. A history on the official Limestone County website says that the small city was flourishing in the early years, but there is no apparent record of why the town was abandoned, what became of the town's structures or why few history books mention the town.

23

OLD CAHAWBA, ALABAMA'S MOST MYSTERIOUS CITY

Note: The spellings "Cahaba" and "Cahawba" are used interchangeably in this story and are used how they are found in corresponding historical references.

The legend of Colonel Christopher Claudius Pegues is one of the most well-known ghost stories in Alabama. The story was a local legend until Alabama's favorite teller of ghost stories, the late Kathryn Tucker Windham, published the story "Spectre in the Maze at Cahaba" in her 1969 book *13 Alabama Ghosts and Jeffrey* and made fans of schoolchildren everywhere.

The tale takes place in Alabama's first capital city, Cahaba.

Pegues was a prominent resident of Cahaba. He was the grandson of Captain Claudius Pegues Jr. (1755–1792), a South Carolina native and an officer in the Revolutionary War. Colonel Pegues moved with his family to Cahaba in 1842 after graduating from college in South Carolina at the age of nineteen. He studied law, was admitted to the state bar in 1845 and soon opened his practice in Cahaba. He married Caroline Coleman, and they built an impressive home, where they raised five children.

When the Civil War began, Pegues joined the Cahaba Rifles, Fifth Alabama Regiment. Within a year, he rose to the rank of colonel. At the Battle of Seven Pines in Henrico, Virginia, after three horses were shot beneath him, Pegues led his regiment by foot before being shot at Gaines Mill on June 27, 1862. Eighteen days later, at the age of thirty-eight, he died from his wounds and is buried in Richmond, Virginia. But Colonel Pegues would soon return to Cahaba in spirit form, according to local legend.

The church looks very much the same today as it did in this undated photo of St. Lukes at Old Cahaba. *Library of Congress.*

The grounds of the Pegues home were known for their beauty and serenity and were dotted with cedars, Lombardy pines, magnolias and soothing fountains. The home was often filled with guests and gaiety. Following Pegues's death, a legend arose that the colonel's spirit had returned to his stately home. The story began one moonlit night in late 1862, when a young couple was out for a romantic stroll in the picturesque grounds behind the Pegues home. They reported that they were walking among the cedars when they saw a "glowing ball of white light," the Old Cahaba Archaeological Site says on its website:

> *Flashing from side to side a few feet above the path, the apparition moved so close that they could almost touch it, then quickly disappeared in the undergrowth only to reappear beside them moments later. When the gentleman tried to touch the object, it disappeared—much like the town itself was soon fated to vanish.*
>
> *The light would appear on other occasions and people wondered if the light, also called a "will o' the wisp," was the specter of Pegues, returned to his beloved home.*

But why? Was he trying to relay a message?

No matter. Cahawba, like the Pegues' Ghost, was soon to become immaterial, a place owing more to the past than the future, a place inhabited primarily by the events of its former glory days. Cahaba would soon become a ghost story itself.

As talks began to carve the state of Alabama from the Mississippi Territory, the soon-to-be state was in need of a capital city. A commission was formed and a site was chosen on land at the confluence of the Alabama and Cahaba Rivers, gifted to the new state by President James Monroe. The future town was named Cahawba. Officially named the state capital in 1819, legislators needed to arrange for a temporary capital while Cahawba was developed, and a site in Huntsville was chosen. This is where legislation formally creating the State of Alabama was ratified.

Cahawba was a fully functioning city as the state capital by the young state's first birthday.

The fact that the city was located in a swampy, remote area between two rivers was a much-argued point among legislators, but Governor William Wyatt Bibb had been able to secure enough votes to get the location approved. The construction and preparation for Cahawba got off to a booming start, and land prices swelled from $1.25 an acre to $60-plus an acre within a year. By 1822, numerous stores, two newspapers, a theater, a state bank, two hotels, two ferries and an imposing two-story brick capitol building had emerged from the swampy ground.

Bad luck soon befell the city, though, as the national economic panic of 1819 finally made its way through Alabama. Many investors lost money on lands and structures they had just acquired in the new city, plunging many into debt. Adding to the debt woes, mosquito-borne diseases spread in the summers of 1821 and 1822, crippling the population growth. In 1822, the Alabama and Cahaba Rivers overflowed their banks after heavy rains and flooded the town. This flood and the unexpected death of Governor Bibb led supporters of moving the capital to Tuscaloosa to make a push for the change.

In 1825, another flood crippled the city, submerging and collapsing part of the statehouse. This was the final straw; on December 13, 1825, a vote passed to move the capital from Cahawba to Tuscaloosa. On February 1, 1826, the move was completed. The populace abandoned the flood-prone city, leaving only three hundred or so people in the former capital. The statehouse and many homes and businesses were abandoned in the six-year-old city.

Having lost its claim as the state capital, Cahawba continued for a time as the seat of Dallas County, and through some hard work, locals were able to rebuild the city's economy. Centered in Alabama's Black Belt region, the city was perfectly located for farmers to ship their goods via the two rivers. The town soon became a major distribution point for cotton shipped down the Alabama River to Mobile for export to Europe. The increase in shipping brought a rail line to the town in 1859, which triggered another explosion of growth. The grand Saltmarsh Hall rose as a site for balls and parties, a female academy was established and many grand homes, such as the Kirkpatrick, Perine and Crocheron residences, were built.

Cahawba had beaten its past and was beginning a new boom time with a population of between three and six thousand when once again the town's fortunes took a turn for the worse.

The year 1861 began a dark time for America and an even darker time for Cahawba. A large cotton warehouse by the new railroad was under construction by local planter and merchant Samuel Hill when the

Shipping down the Alabama River to Mobile was a key to the revitalization of Cahaba in the 1850s. This image of cotton ships in Mobile is a stereopticon photo. *Library of Congress.*

The Perine Well is all that remains of a once great Cahaba home. *Author's collection.*

government of the Confederate States of America ordered the railroad removed for use elsewhere. If this were not damaging enough, the Confederate government requisitioned this unfinished warehouse for use as the Cahaba Federal Prison, which opened in June 1863 to house prisoners of war. The prison grew much too fast and soon had more than 660 prisoners crammed into the fifteen thousand square feet of space in only five months.

Prison surgeon R.H. Whitfield reported poor conditions at the camp:

> *It was an unsanitary water supply entering the compound dirtied by washings of the hands, feet, faces, and heads of soldiers, citizens, and negroes, buckets, tubs, and spittoons of groceries, offices and hospital, hogs, dogs, cows, and horses, and filth of all kinds from the streets and other sources. The building had one fireplace and no bedding or less straw for the mere 432 bunk spaces.*

At its height, the Cahaba Federal Prison, which had garnered the nickname Castle Morgan, housed more than 3,000 prisoners. Shelter, food, water, clothing and even sanitation were almost nonexistent for the prisoners of war and their keepers. Still, federal records indicate that of all the prisoners

A rendering of the Fort Morgan Prison at Cahaba. *Library of Congress.*

A present-day view into one of Cahaba's four cemeteries. *Author's collection.*

A sign asking for respect of the ground of Castle Morgan at Old Cahawba. *Author's collection.*

who made their way through Castle Morgan, only 142 to 147 were reported to have died during their captivity. Today, there are no remains of the prison, but the grassy vacant lot is marked as hallowed ground.

The War Between the States had effectively crushed the town of Cahawba. The cotton business was outright destroyed by the war, the railroad had been removed by the Confederate government, people had fled or been driven out by the war and Castle Morgan seemed to leave a stain on the town. County fathers opted to move the Dallas County seat from Cahawba to Selma in 1866, taking many of the remaining families with it.

By 1870, Cahawba was virtually abandoned, but it would take another 119 years before the town was actually unincorporated.

Much of the town's history remains, including three cemeteries, roadbeds and the ruins of homes and churches. Beginning in 1926, riverboat pilgrimages were implemented to help preserve what was left, and in 1943, the state created the Cahaba Historical Commission to manage preservation projects at the site. Having little funding, the commission was unable to do much. In 1973, the site was added to the National Register of Historic Places, and in 1975, oversight was transferred to the State Historical Commission, which worked to created

Old Cahaba Archeological Site, a tourist attraction today. The park is open to the public, and visitors can take a trip back in time to see the footprint of the state's first capital, walk along the hallowed ground where Castle Morgan once stood, find the few remains of the once bustling city or visit the now-preserved cemeteries.

BIBLIOGRAPHY

Alabama Bigfoot Society. "Recent Sightings." http://alabamabigfootsociety.com/RecentSightings.html.

Alabama Haunted Houses. "Boyington Oak at Church Street Cemetery—Mobile AL Real Haunt." http://www.alabamahauntedhouses.com/real-haunt/boyington-oak-at-church-street-cemetery.html.

———. "Cry Baby Hollow Bridge—Real Haunts in Hartselle AL." http://www.alabamahauntedhouses.com/real-haunt/cry-baby-hollow-bridge.html.

———. "Real Haunt: USS Alabama." http://www.alabamahauntedhouses.com/real-haunt/uss-alabama.html.

AL.com. "Thirteen Places (Including One in Alabama) with Bigfoot Claims to Fame." http://www.al.com/living/index.ssf/2017/02/13_places_including_one_in_ala.html.

Animal Planet. "Finding Bigfoot: Creepy Sounds and Sightings on Creepy Mountain." https://www.animalplanet.com/tv-shows/finding-bigfoot/videos/creepy-sounds-and-sightings-on-creepy-mountain.

Bierce, Ambrose. "Whither?" *San Francisco Examiner*, October 14, 1888. http://anomalyinfo.com/Stories/difficulty-crossing-field-published-1888.

Chattahoochee Heritage Project. "Abbeville Ghosts." http://www.chattahoocheeheritage.org/2012/04/abbeville-ghosts.

Crider, Beverly. "Dead Children's Playground." Strange Alabama. Last modified March 21, 2012. http://blog.al.com/strange-alabama/2012/03/dead_childrens_playground.html.

Dispatches from the LP-OP. http://leepeacock2010.blogspot.com.

Edgemon, Erin. "Church Said to Be Haunted Burns in Alabama." AL.com. February 17, 2015. http://www.al.com/news/montgomery/index.ssf/2015/02/church_said_to_be_haunted_burn.html.

Explore Southern History. "Old Cahawba Archaeological Site—Cahaba, Alabama." http://www.exploresouthernhistory.com/oldcahawba.html.

Fandom. "Church Street Graveyard." http://ghosts.wikia.com/wiki/Church_Street_Graveyard.

Felsher, John N. "Vicious Monsters Lurk in Alabama Rivers." *Alabama Living.* http://alabamaliving.coop/article/vicious-monsters-lurk-in-alabama-rivers.

Gadsden Messenger. "Watch Out…There May Be Monsters in the Coosa!" April 18, 2014. http://gadsdenmessenger.com/2014/04/18/watch-out-there-may-be-monsters-in-the-coosa.

Gilbert, Kathy L. "Haunted?" Even Wesleys Heard 'Bumps in the Night'." http://www.umc.org/news-and-media/haunted-even-wesleys-heard-bumps-in-night.

Goodson, Mike. "Strange Sights Spotted along Coosa River." *Gadsden Times,* September 27, 2009. http://www.gadsdentimes.com/article/DA/20090927/News/603211060/GT.

Gore, Leada. "Alabama's Strangeset Unsolved Mystery You've Probably Never Heard Of: Wednesday's Wake Up Call." AL.com, April 29, 2015. http://www.al.com/opinion/index.ssf/2015/04/alabamas_strangest_unsolved_my.html.

Gurley Lions Club. "The Legend of the Lost Gold of Keel Mountain." http://www.contactez.net/gurleyalabama/KeelMountainMadisonCounty.html.

Hardinger, LaRue. "UFO Still Stumping Skeptics, Believers." *Gadsden Times,* March 11, 1989. https://news.google.com/newspapers?id=xWQfAAAAIBAJ&sjid=29QEAAAAIBAJ&pg=4005,1307954&hl=en.

Haunted Places. "Boyington Oak—Church Street Cemetery." http://www.hauntedplaces.org/item/boyington-oak-church-street-cemetery.

———. "Cry Baby Hollow Bridge." http://www.hauntedplaces.org/item/cry-baby-hollow-bridge.

Haunted Rooms. "USS Alabama BB-60 Ghosts, Mobile, Alabama." https://www.hauntedrooms.com/uss-alabama-bb-60-ghosts-mobile-alabama.

Haunting Darkness. "The Ghosts of the USS Alabama." September 2, 2010. http://ghoststoriesandhauntedplaces.blogspot.com/2010/09/ghosts-of-uss-alabama.html.

Huggin' Molly's. "The Legend of Huggin' Molly." http://www.hugginmollys.com/legend.

Jameson, W.C. *Buried Treasures of the Appalachians.* Little Rock, AR: August House Publishers, 1991.

Kazek, Kelly. "Are There 9,000 Unmarked Graves in Huntsville Slave Cemetery? Historians Intend to Find Out." AL.com. Last modified July 29, 2015. http://www.al.com/living/index.ssf/2015/07/are_there_9000_unmarked_graves.html.

———. "Car-Sized Catfish? Supernatural Serpents? 'Monster Fish' Host Zeb Hogan Discusses Alabama's Legendary River Creatures." AL.com. June 26, 2013. http://www.al.com/living/index.ssf/2013/06/car-sized_catfish_supernatural.html.

———. "Five Mythical Creatures the Reportedly Roam Alabama's Back Roads." AL.com. Last modified March 3, 2018. http://www.al.com/living/index.ssf/2013/10/5_mythical_creatures_that_repo.html.

———. "Mystery Graves of North Alabama Found Home in New Hope (Odd Travels)." AL.com. October 31, 2012. http://www.al.com/living/index.ssf/2012/10/mystery_graves_of_north_alabam.html.

———. "Nine of Alabama's Spookiest Cemeteries." AL.com. October 15, 2014. http://www.al.com/living/index.ssf/2014/10/9_of_alabamas_spookiest_cemete.html.

———. "Nine Weird Facts about Huntsville Learned at the Maple Hill Cemetery Stroll." AL.com. Last modified October 19, 2015. http://www.al.com/living/index.ssf/2015/10/9_weird_facts_about_huntsville.html.

———. "Original Drawing of Legendary Wolf Woman of Mobile Discovered in Archives." AL.com. October 20, 2015. http://www.al.com/living/index.ssf/2015/10/original_drawing_of_legendary.html.

———. "Ten Alabama Urban Legends that Haunted Our Childhoods." AL.com. Last modified October 28, 2017. http://www.al.com/living/index.ssf/2015/06/10_alabama_urban_legends_that.html.

———. "Twenty-Five Years Ago, UFO Hunters Descended on Tiny Alabama Town in Wake of UFO Sightings." AL.com. February 19, 2014. http://www.al.com/living/index.ssf/2014/02/25_years_ago_ufo_hunters_desce.html.

———. "The Witch Legend Behind Huggin' Molly's, the Alabama Eatery with Movie Collectibles." AL.com. February 1, 2017. http://www.al.com/entertainment/index.ssf/2017/02/the_witch_legend_behind_huggin.html.

Kleen, Michael. "Church Street Graveyard's Boyington Oak." Mysterious Heartland. December 3, 2014. https://mysteriousheartland.com/2014/12/03/church-street-graveyards-boyington-oak.

Matthews, Dana. "Dead Children's Playground Is a Haunted Park Hidden Inside Alabama's Largest Cemetery." Week in Weird. June 9, 2016. http://weekinweird.com/2016/06/09/dead-childrens-playground-is-a-haunted-park-hidden-inside-alabamas-largest-cemetery.

Mythical and Paranormal Realm. "The Vanishment of Orion Williamson." April 8, 2012. http://mythical-and-paranormal-blog.blogspot.com/2012/04/vanishment-of-orion-williamson.html.

Native Languages of the Americas. "Legendary Native American Figures: Pukwudgie." http://www.native-languages.org/pukwudgie.htm.

Old Cahawba. http://cahawba.com.

Only in Your State. "This Spooky Small Town in Alabama Could Be Right Out of a Horror Movie." September 10, 2016. http://www.onlyinyourstate.com/alabama/spooky-small-town-al.

Our Valley Events. https://ourvalleyevents.com.

Paranormal Pastor. "The Wolf Woman of Mobile Alabama." August 19, 2009. http://theparanormalpastor.blogspot.com/2009/08/wolf-woman-of-mobile-alabama.html.

Paranormal Site. "The Wolf Woman of Mobile." March 4, 2017. http://theparanormalsite.com/2017/03/the-wolf-woman-of-mobile.

Saint Bartley Primitive Baptist Church. "Church History." http://www.saintbartleypbchurch.org/history.html.

Sargeant, Frank. "Catzilla Prowls the Tennessee River—Monster Catfish Common Catches." AL.com. December 16, 2010. http://www.al.com/sports/index.ssf/2010/12/catzilla_prowls_the_tennessee.html.

Silverfoxfire_ok. "The Vanishment of Orion Williamson." Reddit. https://www.reddit.com/r/UnresolvedMysteries/comments/38rked/the_vanishment_of_orion_williamson.

USS Alabama Battleship Memorial Park. "USS Alabama." http://www.ussalabama.com/explore/uss-alabama-battleship.

Wikipedia. "Boyington Oak." Last modified July 24, 2017. https://en.wikipedia.org/wiki/Boyington_Oak.

———. "Cahaba, Alabama." Last modified May 22, 2018. https://en.wikipedia.org/wiki/Cahaba,_Alabama.

———. "Fyffe, Alabama." Last modified May 2, 2018. https://en.wikipedia.org/wiki/Fyffe,_Alabama.

———. "Maple Hill Cemetery (Huntsville, Alabama)." Last modified October 6, 2017. https://en.wikipedia.org/wiki/Maple_Hill_Cemetery_(Huntsville,_Alabama).

———. "Oakey Streak Methodist Episcopal Church." Last modified December 27, 2017. https://en.wikipedia.org/wiki/Oakey_Streak_Methodist_Episcopal_Church.

———. "Pukwudgie." Last modified May 20, 2015. https://en.wikipedia.org/wiki/Pukwudgie.

———. "USS *Alabama* BB-60." Last modified May 21, 2018. https://en.wikipedia.org/wiki/USS_Alabama_(BB-60).

Woolheater, Craig. "Mysterious 'White Thing' Haunts Residents for Generations." Cryptomundo. November 5, 2006. http://cryptomundo.com/bigfoot-report/white-thing.

XL-Pro Pro. "I Found Keel Mountain Gold." http://www.treasurenet.com/forums/treasure-legends-alabama/98741-i-found-keel-mountain-gold.html.

YouTube. "The Ghost of Huggin' Molly (Abbeville, AL)." Two Egg TV. October 18, 2015. https://www.youtube.com/watch?v=zDdgmuawQeA.

ABOUT THE AUTHOR

Wil Elrick hails from Guntersville in the northeastern part of Alabama. He is a writer and weirdologist who loves telling stories, whether as a tour guide to historic Huntsville or with friends around a campfire. He can often be found off the beaten path researching historical, weird or unusual tales. From time to time, he can even be found participating in a ghost investigation, a Bigfoot hunt or a search for buried treasure. He previously coauthored the book *Alabama Scoundrels: Outlaws, Pirates, Bushwhackers and Bandits* (The History Press, 2014).

Visit us at
www.historypress.com